Saving Green by Going Green

Nancy Zavada, Amy Spatrisano & Shawna McKinley

Simple Steps to Sustainable Meetings
Industry workbooks for strategic planning

MeetGreen®

Saving Green by Going Green
Simple Steps to Sustainable Meetings

© 2011 by Nancy Zavada, Amy Spatrisano, Shawna McKinley

MeetGreen® and its logo are owned by MeetGreen® Inc. All rights reserved. This book may not be reproduced, in whole or in part, including illustrations, in any form (beyond the copying permitted by Sections 107 and 108 of the U.S. Copyright Law and except by reviewers for the public press) without written permission from the publishers.

Printed in the United States of America.
Printed on 100% post-consumer recycled content paper.

Library of Congress Control Number: 2011928331
ISBN: 978-0-9835975-0-6

First Edition

Preface

One of the age-old myths surrounding green meetings is that they are too expensive. Even with a plethora of data to support the cost effectiveness of green meetings, there are many who believe it costs green to be green. This workbook is dedicated to debunking this myth.

If you have picked up this workbook, you may already be greening your meetings or want to better understand how to save money in doing so. The inspiration for writing this workbook and sharing tips and tools is to provide evidence to support the reality that green meetings actually can and do save you money.

The information included here is based on real-life, practical experiences. Although we acknowledge that some green practices can cost more to implement, we know that when assessing a budget in its entirety green meetings reduce costs and save money overall. Green meetings are simply smart business.

By no means are all the ways you can save money by being green captured in this workbook. Our intention is that reading this workbook, adopting the ideas and strategies, and utilizing the tools will prove to you that implementing green meetings really can save you money. We encourage you to take the knowledge you gain and expand on it. Find your own ways to maximize your greening efforts and make them financially rewarding.

Acknowledgments

We would like to thank Oracle, the Unitarian Universalist Association, the Green Meeting Industry Council, the Eclipse Foundation, Fairmont San Francisco, the Canadian Tourism Commission, and the San Francisco Hotel Collaborative for the generous use of case studies highlighting the green accomplishments and savings from their events. We would further like to express our gratitude to the many clients who have allowed us the honor of bringing sustainability and its business case to life at their events.

We would also like to acknowledge the MeetGreen® staff – Cija Huntley, Mary Cameron, Britta Ehnebuske, Carole Garner, Beverly Garzon, Della Green, Rebecca Mebane, and Vanessa Adelmann – for their efforts and dedication, making this book and the stories and learning within it possible.

Table of Contents

I.	Introduction	1
II.	Plan	3
III.	Do	14
IV.	Measure	34
V.	Conclusion	45
VI.	Worksheets	46
VII.	Checklists	54
VIII.	Links/Resources	73
IX.	Glossary	75
	Authors	93
	Company Information	94

Introduction

Although this workbook is slanted toward the planner's perspective around saving money by greening meetings, suppliers too will find useful information about how to calculate savings and examples of what some of their counterparts have done. Anyone who is implementing or plans to implement green meetings will benefit by reading this workbook and using the tools provided. In fact, we suspect that most of you will save far more money by reading this book and adopting what you learn than the cost of buying it!

This workbook is designed to substantiate the belief that green meetings save you money. It takes you through all the stages of planning a meeting. You will find interwoven throughout the sections real-life case studies and actual financial results. Three main sections divide the workbook: Plan, Do and Measure. Included throughout are useful checklists, spreadsheets and formulas that are interwoven in the appropriate sections ready for you to input your own data.

The Plan section begins by describing what to integrate in the planning phase of the event, which is to say before the event happens and is executed. The section deals with organization commitment around sustainability, what questions to ask, the level of corporate engagement and how those relate to greening your meeting.

Naturally, budget is a large portion of the Plan section and includes details about sponsors, grants, government funding, and vendor partnerships. Human resources are also a key element as is the consideration of time and ultimately finding the right balance.

The Do section is the meat of the workbook. Procurement is the essential factor in ensuring and capturing cost reductions. This section uses the framework of rethink, reduce, reuse and recycle in detail in a methodical approach to using procurement practices to maximize results. Included are suggestions about where, when and how to hold your meetings, and it offers fresh ways to reduce costs. Real-life case studies and saving results are described throughout.

The Measure section completes the planning process by illustrating the value and importance of measuring and reporting. If you have done all the steps in the Plan and Do sections and stop there, you will have missed the essential step of recording and reporting your cost savings, which is essential to realizing your results. Four steps are covered in this section and include details about setting your baseline for comparison, selecting what indicators you're using, establishing targets and communicating your results. This section is filled with spreadsheets and formulas to help you capture your data and share your results.

An important note about the use of terminology throughout this workbook: You will discover as you read this workbook that the terms "events" and "meetings" are used interchangeably. We made a conscious choice to do so as the practices discussed throughout this book can be applied to a meeting or an event.

In addition, for the purposes of this workbook, sustainable, environmentally and socially responsible events are included in the term "green events." For MeetGreen®, green events integrate and balance the economic, environmental and social effects of the event throughout all the stages of the planning process in an effort to enable future generations to meet their own needs.

> **APEX Glossary**
>
> **Event:** *An organized occasion such as a meeting, convention, exhibition, special event, gala dinner, etc. An event is often composed of several different yet related FUNCTIONS.*
>
> **Meeting:** *An event where the primary activity of the participants is to attend educational sessions, participate in discussions, social functions, or attend other organized events. There is no exhibit component. Compare with Convention, Exhibitions, Trade Show, Consumer Show.*

LEARNING OBJECTIVES

Our intention is that after completing this workbook you will be able to:

1. Define the resources needed to implement a successful event sustainability plan.
2. Set the scope of the plan.
3. Balance your event budget with a green perspective.
4. Analyze your supply chain to identify specific opportunities to reduce costs while aligning with environmental, social and economic goals.
5. Demonstrate tactics for measuring and benchmarking cost avoidance and reduction.
6. Identify opportunities to make money with the sustainable approach.
7. Track the financial savings to report to and share with key players.

We begin with the initial concept and planning stage of greening your meeting and saving money.

SECTION

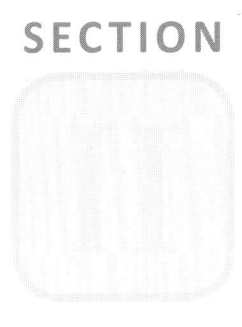

PLAN

You've heard the saying don't bite off more than you can chew. Well, be careful to not do the same with your green meeting. When determining a plan to save money and help the earth, you need to know what resources you have in order to decide what scope of action is feasible. And when we say resources, we're not just talking about money and the trees it grows on. We're also talking about you and your team. Your time is a precious resource, so make sure you plan for how much of it you want to spend researching and implementing your cost-savings green options.

Every meeting starts with a plan. Even before starting the plan there are a series of questions to be asked: Why is the meeting being held? What is the vision? What will participants learn? How will the experience change or motivate the participants? What is the company's return on investment? And so on. Sustainable meetings are no different — they start with the same questions and expand on them.

Organizations that practice sustainable meetings often ask the following:

- How can my company be seen as a good corporate citizen?
- What can we do to minimize our impact on the environment?
- What resources can we allocate for this effort?
- How much time do I have?
- What is reasonable for me to expect to accomplish?
- How prepared and available are my staff and vendor team to help out?

Your answers to these questions will help determine your available resources and identify the scope of action for you to take. The resources to produce a meeting are the same ones you will need to produce it sustainably — organizational support, money, human resources and time.

ORGANIZATIONAL SUPPORT

Gaining the support of your organization first is vital. Start by finding out the degree to which your organization supports sustainability. Without an early understanding of the commitment level, your ability to be successful will be limited. We work with a wide variety of organizations to produce their conferences and events. Although we institute green meeting practices whenever possible in their events — which is how we do business — their commitment in supporting sustainable practices will drive the depth to which utilizing those practices is possible. Here are a few examples of our experiences with clients at different levels of engagement in and perceptions of sustainable meetings to give you an idea of what you may encounter in your own organization.

> Years ago, we had a client who wanted to use our firm because of the depth of our understanding of their industry and its constituents. They were not particularly interested in our environmental expertise, at least not initially. We talked to them early in the planning process about implementing green meeting practices. They agreed to let us implement any practices that did not cost them any money; green practices had to be cost neutral or a cost savings to them. They were also concerned that changes would negatively impact the participants' experience, so were not willing to risk implementing things that might compromise this.

> Another client didn't want to institute any green meeting practices at all, but was willing to sign a large check for carbon offsets to mitigate their impact on the environment. It took many discussions about the risks presented by adopting this approach before they finally understood the importance of reducing first.

> Still another client wanted to be a leader in their industry. They wanted desperately to show competitors how their meeting could be the very "greenest." They were willing to put resources of time, money and expertise behind this goal. They were also willing to drive demand in the hospitality industry by making critical decisions about venue, transportation, and general service contractors based on their ability to also push the envelope of green meeting practices.

And there are, of course, many organizations that fall in between these scenarios.

You may find yourself in a very difficult situation as you move forward with venues and suppliers. Usually, this results because they have the perception that greening may be a drain on resources rather than a resource-generating practice. Sometimes sustainability requires new procedures and practices, and change can be tough for some organizations until they see the positive contributions that can be made by it. When this happens, it is important to engage your colleagues in discussing their goals and how to use resources to maximize returns for all stakeholders. This isn't to say as an individual — passionate about the environment or social justice — your role isn't to push for change. Do push for change and be aware of what resources and backing you have.

Commitment Level Checklist

Use this form to inventory how committed your organization is to holding a sustainable event. Consider what strategies might help to increase support for sustainable practices.

1. How interested are the following in sustainability?	Very uninterested	Uninterested	Neutral	Interested	Very interested
Stockholders					
Senior Management					
Middle Management					
Employees					
Members (if applicable)					
Sponsors (if applicable)					
Vendors					
Me					
Others (if applicable)					

2. For those stakeholders who are interested in sustainability, why are they interested? What attracts them?

3. For those stakeholders not interested in sustainability, what makes them that way? What repels them?

4. Is the organization:	Yes	No
Willing to spend extra time to be green?		
Willing to be green but not spend additional time?		
Willing to spend money to be as green as possible?		
Willing to be green, but only at no additional cost?		
Only willing to be green if it saves money?		
Interested in practices that reflect well on their image?		
Interested in practices that reduce risk?		
Concerned being green may reduce experience quality?		
Able to devote human resources to greening the event?		

5. Can any of the following be harnessed to help get commitment for your sustainable event?	Notes:
Company or event sustainability policy	
Attendee or sponsor feedback	
Employee support	
Vendor support / products / services	
Positive press coverage / presentation or award opportunities	
Demonstrated cost savings	
Standards / regulations affecting your event	
Risk factors (negative PR, additional costs)	
Other	

See pages 47-48 for a full-size worksheet

To help you assess the commitment level, there is a series of questions to ask senior management.

- Who in the organization is interested in sustainability — senior management, stockholders, middle management, and/or employees?
- Is sustainability being driven by any forces outside the organization?
- What is the commitment level of each of these groups?
- Are they willing to spend time and money to be as green as possible?
- Are they interested in green practices that don't cost extra money?
- Do they want to spend money, but not take any additional time to make it happen?
- Are they concerned that the meeting or event will look different?
- Do they think going green means "granola served on burlap sacks" will be the order of the day?

A good place to start is by reviewing your organization's mission or vision statement. Look for statements about the environment or being a good corporate citizen. Other key terms include "health," "children," "families" and "next generations." These commitments can show you a path to getting buy-in and prioritizing action. Following are some examples of how our clients have used their missions to enable organizational buy-in.

> A religious association we work with has specific principles it has committed to uphold in everything they do. One of these principles encourages environmental stewardship, opening a door to being green with their meetings as a way to demonstrate action toward this principle.
>
> The CEO of one of our client companies made a public commitment to be a carbon-neutral organization within three years. In order to align with this commitment, the meetings department had to measure emissions impacts and act to reduce where possible and be accountable for unavoidable event emissions through offsets.
>
> Three years ago, we started assisting a major tourism marketing association with their sustainable event initiative. Their destination brand relied heavily on a beautiful, pristine and clean natural environment. Planning their events in an environmentally responsible way was a natural way to maintain brand integrity.

BUDGET

Always a driving force — money. Many organizations count on the funds from conferences and events for the working capital of the organization. All initiatives impacting the bottom line are under scrutiny, as they should be. Now for the good news: Just as the title of the book states, green meetings save money. This is where you can become the hero! You bring to the table both the ability to produce sustainable events AND to save money!

When you look at available funds, consider what you will be spending as well as what you will be saving. Both are critical and important to track. As an example of this, one client began reducing their paper consumption in 2007 and now has two years of conference history available. The number of printed collateral projects was reduced from 26 to 15 pieces, and the size of the printed materials has also steadily decreased. These reductions have resulted in a savings of 1,305 trees since 2007. But we are here to talk about money — the cost savings of paper reductions in 2009 alone was $162,018.

When looking at your line items on the budget, keep in mind alternative sources for revenue as well.

See page 49 for a full-size worksheet

Sponsorship Model

List those expenses associated with sustainable decisions. Identify sponsorship options to offset any extra costs.

Expense Item:		
Jute conference bag	$10,000	
Reusable water bottle	$7,500	
Recycling center signage	$2,000	
Shirts, training and appreciation for Event Green Team	$7,500	
Print/download stations	$10,000	
Certified organic food for breaks	$5,000	
Non-profit exhibit pavilion	$10,000	
Carbon offset	$8,000	
Total		**$60,000**

Revenue Item:		
Green Exhibit Pavilion sponsor	$12,500	
Carbon offset sponsor	$10,000	
Recycling Center sponsor	$10,000	
CyberCafe sponsor	$10,000	
Wellness Break sponsor (2 @ $2,500)	$5,000	
Green event sponsorships (2 @ $10,000)	$20,000	
Total		**$67,500**

NET REVENUE (INDICATOR)		**$7,500**

Sponsors

Sponsors love sustainable meetings — it makes them look good in the eyes of participants as well as the media. Creative thinking will enroll your sponsors and get the budget items covered:

AV — Produce the general session using LED and other energy-efficient lighting and systems. Have the keynote speaker appear virtually, which will save on greenhouse gas emissions and money. Bill the session as a "Sustainable Experience" and enroll a sponsor.

Breaks — Serve fresh, healthy fruits and vegetables instead of soft drinks and cookies. You can even have a yoga instructor lead participants through a few minutes of stretching exercises. Sponsors for the break may even give away reusable water bottles as part of the "Health Break."

Conference Proceedings — Use USB keys instead of printing documents and have the keys sponsored. This is an especially good opportunity, because even if the participant doesn't want the proceedings, chances are they will keep using the thumb drives for quite a while. Sponsors can include promotional material on the drives as well.

Grants and Government Funding

Money is being spent on green jobs and green technology. Research what might be available to offset some of your line items such as transportation, waste hauling or energy efficiency. Find out what is happening in the local community and take advantage. Also consider what your organization might have available in the way of grants. Many companies and associations operate foundations that might designate money to social and environmental responsibility projects that tie into your event or meeting. Information on grants in your country might be found at:

EcoAction Canada: http://www.ecoaction.gc.ca/grantsrebates-subventionsremises/organizations-organisations-eng.cfm

US Federal Grants: http://www.grants.gov/

European Commission Contracts & Grants: http://ec.europa.eu/contracts_grants/index_en.htm

Vendor Partnerships

Vendors are anxious to be sustainable and to build their green reputations. Find out what new products or services they may have available along these lines. Offer to serve as a case study for a reduced fee. Both of your organizations can then publish the outcomes to an industry hungry to learn more about what others are doing. In 2007, the Green Meeting Industry Council, Nexus Collections and MCI partnered to design and create an environmentally responsible conference bag. Their journey is documented in a GMIC-published white paper: http://www.nexuscollections.com/environment.php?article=10.

You get the idea. We will get into specifics of this and really delve into cost-saving measures in the Procurement section.

HUMAN RESOURCES

Event sustainability is as much about people as it is the environment, so be aware of your human resources. Available staff resources should be inventoried to determine if they can support your greening program. Some staff may be naturally inclined or passionate about sustainability and therefore a logical choice for your green team. Other staff may be already stretched thin with existing responsibilities so be sensitive to overloading. Rewards and incentives can be helpful ways to get staff engaged in additional green efforts. Consider instituting a green award in your department, which provides a gift card or other incentive to be green. Provide a fieldtrip post-conference for your team to get out and enjoy nature.

Volunteers often become a vitally important aspect of greening. If you are teaching participants to use a multi-stream recycling system just to discard their morning coffee cup, it often becomes important to have people standing by to help direct them to the best disposal bin. Volunteers can come from a variety of sources including your own organization's student members or volunteer corp. You can also look to local schools that have "Earth Clubs" or ecology programs at local colleges. We have also tapped into community-based environmental organizations, such as Master Recyclers.

Don't forget about grants that might help increase the capacity of your human resources. Many local colleges and universities operate internships and placements that can be funded externally, so ask if schools provide co-op placement grants. At the time of writing, the U.S. Department of Labor is also offering grants to help companies hire to support "green jobs."

TIME

Time is a vital resource when planning green meetings. The earlier in the process green meeting practices are introduced, the better your chances are of having them be successful. This means from the initial contact and request for proposal, questions about how vendors, venues and management practices will be sustainable must be incorporated. This also affects the bottom line because if there is enough time for planning, great, money-saving things can be accomplished!

> For example, we were planning a conference for 1,000 and wanted to have local/organic spinach served as a salad. We enlisted the help of the venue's chef who had strong contacts with local farmers. What we didn't

know until then was that this one meal would use one farmer's entire crop for the entire season. This made it an impossible request. If we had given that chef enough lead time, it may have been possible for the chef to source a variety of farmers and let them know what to prepare for. It also makes it possible to keep the cost down while supporting the local community, as you are not flying in organic spinach at the last minute.

In another example, by allowing enough lead time for exhibitors one organization was able to pool all exhibitor freight destined for a conference on the West Coast. The freight was then shipped by rail making it more eco-efficient and cost effective. This is only possible when you allow time for planning and scheduling to accommodate consolidation.

Allowing enough time is also important when you are determining the key performance indicators you are requesting. We often give vendors a list of what we expect to have measured so there are no surprises during or after the event. Here are examples of requested information:

- What weight of total waste was recycled?
- What percentage of the total meal was locally grown, organic food products?
- How much food was composted?
- How much food was donated to a local food bank?
- How many shuttles were used? How far did they travel? How much fuel was used? Were alternative fuels sourced?
- What percentage of the venue's energy came from renewable energy sources? How much energy was used?
- What percentage of guests used the hotel's towel/sheet reuse program?
- Were there any cost increases or savings for the event from green practices?

FINDING THE RIGHT BALANCE

Sometimes the right decisions are obvious. More often than not, however, taking the right action involves trade-offs and balancing different priorities. When determining what to leave in and out of your greening plan, it can help to set criteria for making decisions. This will help you evaluate options and make the best choices.

Start by collecting a list of possible priorities you and your meeting stakeholders can agree on. Ask your internal team, your management, and your vendors what their goals are, and don't forget your participants! This might include saving money, ensuring attendee satisfaction, providing a high-quality experience, demonstrating exhibitor or sponsor value as well as reducing environmental impacts.

Sound easy? In some instances it can be. Many practices can help us save money and protect the earth while ensuring attendee value. These are real win-win ideas. Take cutting back on printing, for example. Academic and scientific conferences particularly have huge documentation requirements: abstracts and research papers in addition to regular programs. Switching these to online forms saves trees, energy and water. Your attendees will also likely appreciate all materials being e-mailed or uploaded to a Web site or USB key, as these fit nicely in a suitcase! The cost savings of reduced printing typically outweigh any Web hosting fees, and USB keys can be sponsored. That, plus the ability to update materials closer to the event makes for more timely and accurate information!

Sounds perfect, but there can be challenges. Over many years of planning green meetings, we've learned there is rarely a perfect decision. We've found it helpful to weigh the pros and cons of different options by considering costs and benefits overall. Take the choice of conference bags. Eliminating bags can reduce costs while using fewer environmental resources. However, this decision has to be balanced by considering attendee needs and a possible loss in sponsorship revenue or value.

The following table might be helpful when considering which practices you pursue, and the pros and cons of each:

Analysis of the Impact of Sustainable Options

For each action outline the impact in terms of costs, attendee experience, sponsorship, public relations and sustainability.

Action	Cost impact	Attendee impact	Sponsor impact	Promotional impact	Sustainability impact
First three are examples	Indicate specific $ increases or decreases	Describe how the action will affect the event experience	Describe how sponsor benefit might be positively or negatively impacted	Describe the impact in terms of public relations and image	Describe specific environmental or social benefits in terms of energy, water, waste, pollution, community involvement
Eliminating conference bags	Reduce cost for production and shipping $ estimate	Nothing to carry materials in, so will need to advise to BYOB (bring your own bag)	No opportunity for sponsor inserts. Need to explore other avenues to add value, such as web presence, walk-in slides.		Reduced materials use, shipping and emissions.
Local and organic food procurement	Cost neutral up to 25%. Cost more over 25% because of procurement implications for caterer (outside of normal arrangements with contracted provider).	Fresher food that is in season.	None. Possible opportunity to engage a "health break" sponsor to cover the extra cost of more than 25%.		Reduced emissions by sourcing locally. Greater impact on local economy. Healthier attendees.
Reduce size of printed program from book to mini-program and print on recycled content paper.	Cost savings to use less paper. Cost more to print on FSC-certified paper. Cost more to print on CSC-certified paper.	Need to prepare them to expect a smaller program pre-event. May want to have print stations/Internet kiosks to access programs online.	Retain program sponsor. Additional print station sponsor possible.		Reduced paper use translates into trees, water and energy saved.

See page 50 for a full-size worksheet

We encourage you to document these trade-offs wherever possible. The meetings industry is moving more and more toward standardization of sustainable practices. Documentation of issues, priority setting and the rationale for trade-offs is required under programs like BS 8901 and ISO 20121. If your organization has adopted these or other environmental management systems, your documentation of how you set the scope of your green meeting and prioritized resources use can be an added way for you to contribute to these internal sustainability programs. If you are a supplier or an independent planner, this kind of documentation can also help you earn new business. For example, the Vancouver 2010 Winter Olympics and London 2012 Summer Olympics both require meeting professionals to document and engage in these kinds of sustainable practices in order to be rewarded with contracts.

PARTNERING WITH SUPPLIERS

Finding the right balance in your decision making includes how you will communicate and work with your suppliers and vendors to achieve cost savings. For suppliers you have long-term relationships with, this means letting them know what your intentions are. Ask them what they are willing and able to do to support your cost-reduction strategies.

Your initial conversation with them may be a bit sticky because they will be concerned about how those strategies will affect them. It will be important to assure them that you are still interested in working with them (if this is true) and are looking to them to support your efforts. Although you may be reducing costs in some areas, this may open up opportunities to use those savings in a more meaningful way.

The first time we asked a food-and-beverage supplier to eliminate bottled water (at $4.50 plus tax and gratuity per bottle) and provide the large, refillable water containers (offered at the time for free), they were, to put it politely, resistant. However, when they realized we would be using a portion of the savings to offer a more sustainable menu, they were much more willing to comply.

There will certainly be times when you will have to use your negotiating skills to convince a supplier to offer cost-saving elements. As in all good negotiations, be sure to have something in it for them. The benefit to them could be similar to the previous example or additional business opportunities or favorable press or even the supplier's own experience of savings. One of our clients worked with their signage supplier to ensure that a more sustainable material was used for signs. They hadn't yet decided to reduce the number of signs, just to use the more responsible material. As it turned out, the signage material ended up being a less-expensive option for the supplier. So, the supplier's net gain was a positive one.

Your ability to collect the cost-saving figures will depend on three elements. First, whether or not you let the supplier know from the beginning you were going to ask them to provide the data, so they could be prepared to supply it. Second, if you included your expectations in your contract with the supplier requiring the information. Third, if your relationship with a vendor or supplier is a new one, you should be sure to include information in your request for proposal language.

Bear in mind that your supplier partnerships are not just about squeezing cost savings every time. It won't always be possible to directly save money through vendors. Sometimes it's also about leveraging more value from the supply chain to ensure triple-bottom-line approaches can be communicated. These can, in turn, help realize other business benefits that might improve your reputation or leadership position. For example, you may not be able to afford the most energy-efficient audiovisual equipment, but your supplier might be able to better itemize the power savings associated with the equipment they're already using in some applications. These energy savings can give you a good news story that you and your supplier can share in the media, making you both look good while garnering free press!

SECTION III

DO

You're through the initial stage of planning your meeting and well on your way toward implementation. This section is all about the Do part, beginning with procurement. Purchasing is at the heart of your ability to successfully produce a green meeting that will save you money.

PROCUREMENT

As you learned while taking the inventory of your supply chain, there is a very long list of items required for events. The easiest way to determine how to save money is by reviewing each of the items in the supply chain using a framework. The framework is based on rethinking, reducing, reusing and recycling. In this section, we will describe each of these options and give you examples of how the items fit into the framework. This type of analysis can show where trade-offs might be able to be made between things that cost and things that save.

Note: Stop, breathe and remember that you don't have to do all of these things the first time. It is indeed a journey. You may want to pick the items that have the most economic return or are the easiest to do first. As you build momentum for the green program, you can add new items.

As you read through these sections, note that we have told what type of savings was incurred after each example. You will also find the budget items from the supply chain inventory in bold for your quick reference. Now, let's get started.

Icon Key	
$	Financial Savings
⏱	Time Savings
🌿	Environmental Savings
👥	Human Resource Savings

See page 51 for a full-size worksheet

Supply Chain Inventory

This is a basic list of all items typically purchased for a conference. Using this spreadsheet during the planning and budgeting phase will help you make critical decisions to save both money and the environment whenever possible.

Item	Vendor	Sustainability Features / Criteria	Cost Implications
	Who is providing this product/service?	*What kind of environmental or social responsibility criteria does the product/service meet?*	*What are the financial savings or costs of this decision?*
Meeting rooms			
Sleeping rooms			
Airfare			
Ground transportation			
Airport transportation			
Shuttle transportation			
Speaker expenses			
Food and beverage			
Breaks			
Lunch			
Dinner/reception			
Audiovisual/production			
Internet connectivity			
Equipment rental			
General service contractor			
Electronic material production			
Printed materials, printed program, inserts			
Handouts or bag inserts			
Giveaway or promotional items			
Conference bag			
Name badges and supplies			
Pre-registration announcements			
Clerical expenses			
Temp staff or volunteers			
Telephone			
Online registration			
Postage and shipping			
Signage			
Total (above or below budget)			

RETHINK

Haven't we all been rethinking our events lately? We still need to connect, educate and inform our participants — but what is the best way given current economic, societal and environmental considerations? Whether or not you have been using green practices, you have most likely been very strategic in developing your meetings. Rethinking is key, because if there is a way to eliminate it from the beginning, there will be no need to reduce, reuse or recycle it!

Sustainable meeting strategies are just another filter for decision-making strategies that can save you valuable time, money and human resources. Each of the areas listed on the supply chain inventory can be put through this filter by asking a series of questions. The answers to these questions may lead you to decide whether the best strategy is to reduce, reuse or recycle. But it may be the answer is that you really don't need it anymore. Times have changed, participants have changed, expectations of key stakeholders have changed and your organization has changed.

Questions to ask:
- Is it necessary to do this?
- Is there a better way to achieve the same objective?
- Have we reviewed our options in the last six months?
- If the green option costs money, can we recoup that cost somewhere else?
- What other use could it have?
- How will this event reflect the values of my organization?

Examples:

Eliminate specific branding. Think of all of the **signage** and **promotional products** that are imprinted with either the year or branding specific to one event. Typically, the vital information is the sponsoring organization and title of the conference. For example, the Green Meeting Industry Council has produced room signs from sustainable material with a header and border featuring the title of the conference "Sustainable Meetings Conference" and the GMIC logo. There is an area to slip in room session signs made from standard paper. These signs don't have the date or year on them and can (and are) reused each year. Determine your savings by multiplying the number of signs you use each year by the cost of producing one. And then multiply that number by the number of years you will use them in the future. Even for small meetings, there is a significant savings. You can read more about reusing them for other events in the Oracle OpenWorld Case Study in this section.

Cut travel expenses. Before jumping on a plane or requiring others to do so, be clear about what will be accomplished by the trip. One large international conference committee met five times in the destination city before the actual conference for **planning meetings**. Once their budget was slashed, they had to find a way to do it differently. Their solution was to hold the kick-off planning meeting the day after the previous year's conference as they were already together. Their next meeting was held in the destination city at the meeting venue knowing it was important for all of them to see the site and work the flow into their planning process. The next two meetings were then able to be held virtually and meet their objectives. It was important to hold the final meeting at the facility again, but this time it was determined that just the "operational" committee members would attend physically and the others would participate virtually. This cost-saving solution minimized the need for **airfare, meeting rooms** and **sleeping rooms**, saving both the environment and time for the busy volunteer committee members. Don't forget to save on **telephone** and **long distance charges** by using a technology like Skype or GoToMeeting.

Connect virtually. As technology improves daily and the cost comes down, it becomes possible to meet expectations without ever leaving home. We see examples of this with virtual trade shows, which expand opportunities for exhibitors and sponsors while letting participants engage without ever stepping foot away from their offices. The bonus is the ability to gain a larger audience from those who may not have been able to attend because their travel budgets have been cut.

Another interesting new concept is that of hybrid meetings. Hybrid meetings, as the name implies, include both virtual and face-to-face opportunities. Opportunities to connect and learn. In one model, a group meets in a city with a speaker in the traditional fashion. What isn't traditional is that the speaker (and many times the audience) are then broadcast to several other sites in different cities where groups are gathered. This allows for face-to-face connection by the participants in each city plus the virtual gathering and presentation, saving on airfare as well as **meeting rooms** and **sleeping rooms**. If the speaker comes in virtually too, this will save on **speaking fees** and **speaker expenses**. We are finding speakers all too willing to give up life on the road for the opportunity to speak from a local site.

Many hospitality industry suppliers and some planners react with fear when they hear about virtual meetings. There are still roles for both of these groups in virtual meetings; it is important to determine what those are. For example, hotels and convention centers should become the locations for these events. Moving forward, facilities will need to have the technology resources to serve as a downlink site or broadcast site for both large meetings and small, boardroom meetings. Meeting planners should learn about virtual meeting technology and create a new skill set. After all, someone will still need to coordinate the program and speakers, invite and manage the participants, enroll the sponsors, etc. It just looks different from the traditional meeting.

Eat well. Watch the **food-and-beverage** industry trends and you will see quickly that what people want is fresh, healthy food. They are asking for local, organic fare and enjoy knowing where it is coming from. In addition to being good for your body, it is also good for the environment and the local community. Get back to basics. In Portland, Oregon, the local newspaper investigated three examples associated with delivering a pound of fresh blueberries to points of sale.

1. **Air freight from Chile. You pay about $18 per pound** (berries typically come in 4.4 ounce containers and sell for $5.) This does not include customs clearance or ground handling on arrival in the U.S., which could add 20 cents a pound to the cost.

2. **Ground transportation. You pay about $3.50 per pound.** This is based on a refrigerated trailer traveling within 100 miles following major multiple-retailer channels to the point of sale.

3. **Local farmers market direct delivery. You pay about $2.50 per pound.** This is based on a shipment originating 20 miles away traveling in a non-refrigerated pickup truck. (The Oregonian, Sunday, August 10, 2009)

Saving money can come from simple ideas like serving whole fruit instead of paying additional money for the labor to produce sliced fruit platters or having an iced tea and lemonade break served out of colorful pitchers instead of individual cans of soda and bottled water.

Ask the chef to work with you on a hearty vegetarian meal (not just steamed veggies over rice). We have found the cost savings to be about 20% from meals that contain meat. Chefs are usually quite happy to be off the standard banquet menu working creatively to develop a new dish. Even the meat eaters in your group won't complain when there isn't another rubber chicken staring up at them from the plate.

Forgo traditional name badges. There are a lot of great options for environmentally friendly and now cost-effective **name badges**, which we will talk about in the next section. But just for a minute, think about what else you may be able to use. If your organization or event participants already have name badges — as in the case of realtors — is there any reason for another name badge? Wouldn't it be great if they just showed off their own?

One group decided that instead of the plastic cover, lanyard, etc. they would print the paper name badge and then let participants affix it with a lapel pin of the organization's logo. This lapel pin could be worn long after the event and the paper badges held up just fine to four days of wear and tear. This was a much cheaper, green solution and there was no labor needed to stuff the name badges into the holders.

Cut temporary staff hours. Labor costs are high and minimizing staff time whenever possible directly impacts your bottom line. Many of the other items you rethink will also save human resources. Like the example of not stuffing badges into holders, if you don't have a **conference bag** or minimize the **inserts**, you will save time not collating and stuffing them. Using kiosks for **online, on-site registration** saves on registration desk personnel. And not producing **handouts** not only saves on paper, but also saves the time on-site needed to either print or unpack them, get them to the right room and into people's hands and recycle them afterward.

Case studies:

Unitarian Universalist Association Eco-Event Zone Provides Cost Efficiencies
If you've ever watched shows move in and out of an exhibit hall, you may have thought to yourself: Why don't they just use the same carpet and setup? Wouldn't it be easier and cheaper? In a very innovative move, UUA cooperated with the Presbyterian Church General Assembly to reduce their mutual event footprints by agreeing to work with the same general service contractor over back-to-back events. Collaboration in planning allowed both organizations to save setup fees and eliminate freight shipping by using the same carpet, drape and room layouts across their General Assemblies, held one after the other in Minneapolis. Financial savings were estimated at $3,700.

Oracle OpenWorld Signage
Oracle OpenWorld could be accused of painting the town red. If you've ever visited San Francisco in the fall while their event is on, it's hard to miss. The Oracle brand is very strong and consistent, and strengthened when generic event branding enables reuse of signs and cost savings. Since starting their event sustainability initiative in 2008, Oracle has saved $420,000 by rethinking signage. Cost-saving measures have been supported by vendors such as Hartmann Studios and Champion Expositions, which are following expectations set by Oracle to reduce impacts and costs where possible. Tactics to cut costs have included:

- Shifting to lighter substrates made from renewable paper-based resources.
- Designing costlier, larger graphics such as banners and tenting for reuse.
- Reducing the total amount of signage produced.
- Using suppliers in California to reduce cross-country shipments.

REDUCE

When you reduce, the savings are always economic as well as environmental. Using less resources saves money and it is amazing how much can be saved by reducing without affecting the quality of the event. Always look to reduction before reuse and recycling in your planning process. In this section, we give you a lot of examples and case studies from real, live events to stimulate your thinking on what might be possible in your organization.

Questions to ask:
- How can we reduce the stuff we use?
- Can we do without this to reduce our overall ecological footprint?
- How will this reduction affect the event?
- Will reducing this save money, time and resources?
- Do the benefits outweigh any concerns?
- Can I find this locally to save freight costs?

Examples:

Reduce printed materials on-site. This is probably the easiest area to take on first and get some early successes. Start by taking an inventory of all the **printed materials** participants receive. Is there a way to combine some of these documents or eliminate them altogether? If not, take a look at reducing the size and amount of paper required. One conference saved 965 trees by reducing the size of their printed **program**. They saved economically as well, but the CEO announced this reduction by giving the tree statistic during the opening general session and received a huge response from the audience. Not a bad way to start the event.

Exhibitors often have **fliers** in the **conference bag** as one component of their sponsorship package. Event producers are now downsizing the ad size combining them into one flier if they can't eliminate them or include them on the conference USB key.

This leads us to the topic of how to handle proceedings or conference-related handouts. Academic and technology conferences are moving to providing this information electronically either on a Web site or USB key. This has become much more widely accepted over the past few years. But there is still push back in some sectors and reluctance to change. If going "cold turkey" is too much for your organization, there are ways to wean participants from paper. One option is to give them the choice between receiving the information electronically or on paper and reducing the number of handouts printed (duplex, please). Now, if dangling the carrot doesn't work, here is the stick — charge for the paper copies. It turns out that money talks and those who complain loudly about not having paper **handouts** are actually not willing to pay more for them.

On-demand printing stations are also an option. They can either print **handouts** at kiosks by themselves or have a desk at registration where participants can order paper handouts. Have student volunteers manage this process and charge for the service. Participants get their paper and the students get the profit from this printing for their scholarship or activity fund.

Just one note of caution here — when you are able to go paperless both in printed materials on-site and preconference communication, don't think that you are done incorporating green meeting practices. There is often the feeling that this is a good place to stop and you have a green event. It is actually just the first step toward a green meeting, so applaud yourself for a job well done and look for the next opportunity.

Communicate electronically. This area has changed drastically over the past few years and doesn't require a lot of discussion. People are much more willing to communicate electronically now and have embraced social media to keep connected. Their acceptance makes your job easier. No longer do you need to mail promotional information, registration confirmation, schedules, etc. Several years ago, one of our staff registered for a conference and received over eight pounds of fliers, invitations, etc. related to the conference before leaving. Thankfully, when registering for the same event this year, most of the information came electronically.

This should apply to all of your vendors as well. You should receive rooming lists, **exhibitor kits, banquet event orders** and diagrams electronically. Gone are the days of receiving two inches of faxed BEOs, which you sign and fax back creating even more paper. If those days are not gone, it is time to ask your vendors to update their systems.

When you are tracking the savings for this category, keep in mind all of the different areas it affects. For example, not mailing **name badges** saves postage and staff time preparing the mailing. There are significant savings in both categories. Not printing the **advance program** saves on design, printing, paper, postage, and many times, mailing house costs.

Reduce or eliminate conference bags and promotional items. Before you think of all of the reasons you cannot eliminate **conference bags**, think of their cost — purchasing, shipping, stuffing, distributing, to name a few. What if you could eliminate that from your budget? OK, now that we have your attention, let's talk about the options.

Event planners have started asking registrants on their **registration page** if they will need a conference bag. This allows them to decrease the number ordered. One group offered an extra drink ticket for the reception instead of a conference bag. Fifty percent wanted that additional beverage more than a conference bag.

If your conference or event is known for collectible bags, you are a prime candidate for eliminating them this year. Have past participants bring their favorite bag from a past conference or have a contest to see who has the oldest conference bag. In addition, have participants bring a bag that tells others something about them — a favorite vacation spot, hobby, traveling backpack. It becomes a networking activity instead of a disappointment that there is no new bag this year.

Make sure promotional items are relevant and useful. If you are eliminating bottled water, have a sponsor produce a reusable water bottle (coffee mugs too). Re-evaluate your tradition of always including giveaways and consider the USB key with conference information in this category. It can be sponsored, reused, easy to travel with and very useful.

Minimize individual food servings. Serving in bulk saves money and the environment. Caterers we have worked with estimate the savings between 50% and 60% for serving bulk condiments instead of individually packaged. Always require that **coffee and tea service** condiments be served in bulk. We have already talked about another couple of options in bulk service with beverages and fruit, but what happens if you need to serve box lunches? Sometimes it is just a necessity, but there are always options. Start by coming up with a creative way to replace the container. One event employed sponsored carpenters aprons for a container; another had bags available if needed, but most people just grabbed a sandwich and an apple and off they went. Then try to steer away from as much individual packaging as possible. Have participants put mustard, mayo, etc. on their sandwiches before wrapping them up. **Cookies and whole fruit** don't require packaging and also don't require utensils. You get the idea, meet with the chef and get creative. Ask the caterer to pass along some of the savings by lowering the cost of the meal.

Choose a walkable destination. The choices you make when choosing your event destination will have considerable impact on your event's economic and environmental bottom line. Events that are held in locations served by mass transit and within walking distance of **restaurants, activities,** and **sleeping rooms** save you money. There is no need for shuttles, rental cars or taxis — all of which cost you or your participants money. To ensure this is readily adopted, inform participants of environmentally responsible **transportation** options. Use your communications (such as the registration confirmation e-mail) to tell them the best way to get from their airport to the hotel to the convention center. Give them pedometers (sponsorship opportunity) and have a contest for the most miles walked. Make it fun!

If **shuttles** cannot be avoided, minimize the **shuttle** times and area covered to save time and the environment (e.g., don't shuttle for distances less than six blocks), but do have **transportation** available for those with special needs.

When using a transportation company, request their environmental policies as part of the RFP process. Require the use of alternative fuels (biodiesel, electric, ethanol, natural gas) or hybrid vehicles and avoid unnecessary idling. Put it in the contract!

Reduce shipping, buy or rent locally. In all of your purchases and rentals — go local. **Shipping** and **freight** are expensive and costly to the environment. Work with your general contractor to get all equipment rentals from a source close to the event location. Ask exhibitors to do the same. **Audiovisual** and **production equipment** don't have to come from across the country and can be rented locally. Even if your A/V production company travels with you to various cities, they should be able to get the equipment and most of the labor locally without sacrificing the quality of the event. As a quick reminder, also look for local talent!

If you are printing, find a local environmental printing company. For a recent international conference, we stopped printing in our city and then **shipping** overseas by going several days early to the meeting location and working with a local community. Not only does this help the local economy but it also stops the customs headaches.

Reduce energy consumption of production. Save money on your **electrical costs** by choosing a robust low-energy lighting package for your main stage or **exhibit booth**. Your electrical requirements will be reduced significantly: The more LED and HID units your A/V provider is able to substitute into your lighting scheme, the less power you will need.

In venues where electricity is charged by the watt or service size, this can amount to thousands of dollars in savings. EXAMPLE: For a 36-light system using conventional 575-1000 watt fixtures, your power needs (100 amps, 3-phase, 120/208-volt) would average about $1,000. For the same system in LED, your power needs (three 20-amp 120-volt outlets) would average about $225. Please note that these charges may vary depending on the venue — but you get the idea.

Case studies:

EclipseCon Refresh Stations

The Open Source Developers Community meets annually at EclipseCon to network, learn, present, and generally burn the candle at both ends. With their requirements for always having both the most up-to-date information and strong black coffee, the "Refresh Station" was born.

Sold as a sponsorship opportunity, an area of the conference was set aside for participants to:

- Refresh their USB keys (at plug-in stations). Computers were set up to update

the USB keys that were given at registration with the latest information posted by presenters.
- Refresh their bodies with fresh, hot coffee and cookies while resting at tables and chairs.
- Refresh their laptops/cell phones with electrical outlets for recharging. Power strips were available on each of the rounds to fuel the communication.
- Refresh their minds by meeting new people and exchanging ideas at the tables. It was a great gathering spot for old friends and a place to meet with new ones.

The sponsors loved the idea as much as the participants and it gave them great presence in the open source community. The cost of providing the equipment was more than offset by the sponsor dollars, and while it increased the energy usage, it aided those still giving up their precious paper handouts.

Oracle OpenWorld Transportation Plan
With over 40,000 attendees and 80 host hotels, elimination of shuttles is a nonstarter at Oracle OpenWorld. There are just too many people trying to get to too many venues to trust attendees will get where they need to be without a comprehensive shuttling plan! That said, careful attention to this aspect by Hartmann Studios has enabled significant reductions in bus use from 2008–2010 that have resulted in no disruption to the attendee experience at the event and — wait for it — half a million dollars in cost savings! This while attendee numbers continue to climb. How'd they do it? Well, it helps to have San Francisco as your host city, with its walkable downtown core and integrated transit system, of course. Specific savings came from:

- Expanding attendee walking routes to hotels.
- Shuttling to local transit nodes rather than from remote areas into downtown.
- Tracking ridership and eliminating certain routes that were poorly used.
- Promoting virtual conferencing, walking, carpool and transit use in planning.

Oracle OpenWorld Paper Savings
In the age of e-mail and social media, very few of us check the mail anymore when we want to know what is going on in the world. As a result, very few events rely on direct mail and save-the-date notices that use old-fashioned snail mail. Some are even doing away with paper-based programs and dailies by exclusively using digital communication. The Oracle OpenWorld experience reminds us that in addition to the convenience it just makes sense to reduce paper use. Improvements to online attendee communications helped strip $11,000 from event budgets in 2008 when online program schedulers were introduced. A further $162,000 was slashed when conference programs and dailies were reduced in 2009. Overall, these efforts have conserved 1,500 trees!

General Assembly Ships Less, Saves More

It's a simple equation — use less, pay less. Between 2009 and 2010 the Unitarian Universalist Association cut the amount of material shipped to their General Assembly of Congregations by 20%. This was done by working with Association ministries pre-event to reduce packing and materials shipped from their headquarters in Boston. The end result? $1,200 saved! Furthermore, shipping reductions have contributed to less waste being produced on-site. Between 2009 and 2010 General Assembly waste dropped by 46%, building on an already impressive 53% reduction in event waste from 2008 to 2009!

Unitarian Universalist Association Walkable Destinations

The first step to being green and saving green for the UUA is selecting an accessible host city. Accessibility means three things:

- People of all physical abilities can get to and from the event without impediment.
- Connections between the airport and convention core must be convenient, close and affordable.
- Distance between the event venue and host hotel must be in close proximity — either easily navigable by foot or other people-powered mobility devices.

All of these things make sense from a social and environmental perspective. Local air quality is improved, and all 3,500 event participants have equal ability to access the event in a dignified way regardless of their physical ability. Choosing a walkable city also saves UUA an estimated $80,000 against budget by preventing the hiring of motor coach transport.

> **APEX Glossary**
>
> **Walkable (ASTM/APEX Standard):** *half mile or shorter walk between the convention center and 50% of conference hotels.*

REUSE

When you are planning a strategy based on reuse, remember it goes both ways. Are the goods and equipment you are using already available for rental and don't have to be made? Are products you are purchasing made from recycled content? Likewise, after the event, are you donating all these products so that they may continue to be reused? Never buy new what already exists. You would be amazed at what is available. There are a variety of Web sites now that sell event items such as decorations, show furniture, linens, centerpieces, etc. that have been used for an event at extremely reasonable prices. Reuse is continuously gaining in popularity, which makes the search much easier.

Questions to ask:
- Can we afford to invest in more durable items that have a longer life span?
- What are the additional costs of doing this (i.e., in terms of storage, shipping)?
- How can we do this internally, and get our vendors and attendees to do the same?
- Who can benefit from our used items?

Examples:

Eliminate disposable plates and cutlery. This is an area where reuse is vitally important to the environment and usually cost neutral to the planner. This statistic from the Environmental Defense Fund really makes this point, "Using 1,000 disposable plastic teaspoons consumes over 10 times more energy and natural resources than manufacturing one stainless steel teaspoon and washing it 1,000 times." In addition, you will not be putting plastic into the landfill of the community where your event is being held.

But there is another reason to eliminate disposables — your organization's image. First of all, participants are watching waste now and will take note of the amount of plastic going into the garbage. Think for a minute about the perception of being served with china. It is a first-class experience. When having a cup of tea in first class on an airline, you are served with a china mug, and it is a much better experience than being served back in coach (the same tea mind you) in a Styrofoam cup. Isn't that what you want your guests to experience?

If for some reason china and silver aren't possible, such as for a large outdoor event, make sure the disposable serviceware is made from recycled material and is compostable. And make sure to compost it along with food waste. Several years ago, the cost of recycled, compostable or biodegradable plates, cups and cutlery was more expensive than their petroleum-based counterparts. But today, thanks to the high price of oil, the cost is comparable or even less. If you get push back from caterers, ask them to source both and have you review the costs. When we did this in 2007, we found a $2,700 savings for one event.

Repurpose conference supplies. The goal is always to order the exact number of any conference supplies, but many times there is an overage. Looking for a local source for donation is important so these supplies are not shipped again or dumped into the landfill. Many school systems have programs that collect extra conference supplies such as conference bags, pens, paper, and even giveaways. Ask either your meeting venue or local convention bureau what donation programs they may be already working with. We have talked about signage already, but don't forget those room signs and large set pieces often find homes with theatre groups. You can take this all the way to the exhibit show floor with donations of wood products to organizations like Habitat for Humanity. Many of these organizations will give your organization a tax donation receipt as well.

Reuse recycled name badges. If you haven't checked your sources for traditional name badge holders in the past six months — check again. Things are moving so quickly in this department you will be pleasantly surprised. We have been working on moving to more sustainable name badge holders for our clients. We are now able to source a biodegradable, compostable and recyclable holder. It is made of a lighter-weight plastic that is perfect for a short-lived event. And — bonus — it was much cheaper than our usual badge that was made of recycled polypropylene. There are so many green options out there for these products, it's really a matter of striking a balance of what will work best for participants, the budget and what is best for the earth.

And then reuse them. Collect name badges at the end of the event for reuse. Most conferences get a 15% to 25% return rate. Recently, a conference offered a (sponsored) iPod drawing for all those who recycled their holders; their rate went to 85% return. Again, the power of dangling the carrot.

Rent equipment and recycled carpet. The exhibit show floor after an event can be a mountain of waste ready to go to the landfill, or the items left behind can be reused, donated, and returned. Look to your general service contractor for the most eco-friendly options available. Promote those options to all exhibitors in their kits and pre-event information. If you can find recycled or reused equipment, use it. If you can build out the show or display units without building new ones, do it. If you can donate whatever items weren't rented, plan to. Remember that conference and event organizers are traditionally charged for the waste hauling fees by the venue. This can amount to a significant cost savings depending upon the scope of your event.

Minimize and then donate leftover food. Before we launch into donating leftover food, let's talk a minute about saving money by guaranteeing numbers as close as possible to the number of guests you will have attending. In the early years, we worked with a software engineering conference that had developed formulas for guarantees that were impeccable (creating formulas — it's what they do). They would have a lunch for a guaranteed number of 1000 people and the actual number sitting down to the meal was always within 5 people. This was frankly scary to watch when they got down to the last few guests, but everyone had a place to sit and a meal to eat.

Their system was simple, keep a history of guarantees and actual numbers for every function including breaks and produce a formula. And build on it with every event. The formula may have been adjusted slightly from year to year if the conference was in an area where there were a lot of yummy local restaurants to entice participants away or if there was absolutely nothing close by. Here's an example of how the daily formula looked:

Start with a number including all of the conference community such as registered participants, staff, speakers, exhibitors, and sponsors who were expected to eat. Calculate the guarantee based on:
- 83% showing up for the continental breakfast before the keynote.
- 90% for the first break (a few latecomers in the morning).
- 85% for lunch.
- 80% were still there at afternoon break.
- 75% attended the evening reception if the refreshments were free and 50% if they weren't.
- By the last day of the conference, the numbers were adjusted into the 60% range.

If you don't have raw data for your event yet, use these numbers to get you started and adjust the formula based on your actual numbers. We have used it with a variety of different groups with great success. The cost savings on the food budget are quite high with close guarantees if you are not paying for extra meals that go uneaten.

Moving on to food donation. This is one area where the urban myth of "Isn't it illegal to donate food after an event? I am told it is against health codes" is slow to die. In today's world where food banks are struggling to fill their shelves to help the hungry, planners want to know how to help. The Bill Emerson Food Donation Act allows you to help the hungry.

What does the law do? The law protects good-faith donors from civil and criminal liability in the event that the product later causes harm to its recipient. The Emerson Act gives uniform protection to food donors who may cross state lines.

Who is protected? The law protects food donors, including individuals and nonprofit feeding programs that act in good faith. More specifically, the law protects individuals, corporations, partnerships, organizations, associations, governmental entities, wholesalers, retailers, restaurateurs, caterers, farmers, gleaners, nonprofit agencies and others.

What sort of food is protected? The Emerson Act provides protection for food and grocery products that meet all quality and labeling standards imposed by federal, state, and local laws and regulations — even though the food may not be readily marketable due to appearance, age, freshness, grade, size, surplus or other conditions.

Where can I get a copy of the law? For a copy of the Bill Emerson Food Donation Act, check out: http://www.usda.gov/news/pubs/gleaning/appc.htm

Where can I find a place to donate? Find a local food bank using the locator on Feeding America (formerly Second Harvest) http://www.feedingamerica.org/ Your role is to connect the local food bank and the catering firm. They will take care of the details.

In addition, food banks will give you receipts for your donation for tax purposes. Push back when you encounter resistance from caterers. And you will.

Case studies:

The San Francisco Hotel/Non-profit Collaborative

Hoteliers are always aware of the need to "maintain their assets," which generally is taken to mean taking care of the property. To this end, hotels put great effort and expense into frequent upgrading of rooms, public spaces and other facilities. All of this remodeling and refurbishing typically results in huge amounts of material that ends up being discarded and ultimately sent to landfills. Also destined for landfills are the collateral materials left behind at hotels after events — visors, cups, coffee mugs, notepads, pens, tote bags, and an endless stream of other promotional materials.

Luckily for San Francisco's over-taxed landfill, our depleting natural resources, and for the rest of us, a small group of San Francisco hoteliers have been busy supporting the community and saving the environment, all while maintaining their assets AND helping the bottom line for good measure.

The San Francisco Hotel/Non-profit Collaborative was cofounded over 15 years ago by Jo Licata, Community Projects Manager at the Hilton San Francisco Union Square (who continues to organize and maintain it). The other component of the membership was nonprofit organizations — some of the best and most reputable groups serving the San Francisco community. Glide Memorial Church, Street, and St. Anthony's were among the earliest members. There are now almost 20 large properties, as well as the Moscone Center and other hospitality businesses and well over 20 nonprofit organizations that meet on a monthly basis as part of the Hotel/Non-Profit Collaborative.

The goal of the Collaborative is to take usable discards from the waste stream of hospitality organizations and divert them into a steady stream of in-kind support for the nonprofit agencies. Each year through the Collaborative hundreds of tons of materials are diverted from our landfills. Nonprofit agencies receive desks and beds; at-risk children receive school clothes and toys; re-entry workers receive clothing; children in the Tenderloin receive a chance to learn computer skills — it would be impossible to recount all of the benefits to the community from these small efforts. But one more benefit worth mentioning here is the reduced garbage costs to the businesses. Throwing away all those beds, sofas, foam-core signs and giveaways costs money in labor and garbage bills. Donating them to worthy causes not only saves money by making the problem "go away," it also goes a long way in creating a positive spirit of giving throughout the organization.

The Feel-good and Financial Returns of Donating

Sometimes ideas for cost savings come back in unexpected ways. Following a few years of use at Canada Media Marketplace, event organizers needed to retire some furnishings from their 2009 event held at the Waldorf-Astoria in New York. The inventory included tables and chairs that were in perfectly good condition, but would be costly to continue to store and ship when it was likely changes in event branding would make them redundant the next year. Not content to landfill them, organizers hooked up with Furnish a Future to donate the furniture. This program provides formerly homeless families in the New York area with free furnishings for their new dwellings. Not only could organizers reduce cost by eliminating shipping post-event, they could also receive a charitable tax receipt for the value of the furniture, estimated at $1,000."

RECYCLE

Recycling is the final option before the landfill and one that can still have an impact on your economic bottom line. It is essential to the environmental bottom line and cannot be stressed enough. It is also becoming one of the easiest to request and implement. It is important to note that even if a meeting or event venue says they recycle, more questions need to be asked including:
- What do you recycle (paper, plastic, glass, metal, kitchen grease)?
- Do you recycle facilitywide (and not just in the sales office)?
- What is your diversion rate?
- Can you show me the recycling system back of house? This is probably the most important question. Make sure you see exactly how it is handled.

During 2008–2009, 91% of the hotels used by MeetGreen® clients were able to recycle during their events. The minimum waste produced per attendee was 1.5 lbs. The average waste produced per attendee for these events was 4.4 lbs.

Questions to ask:
- How can recycling this save us money?
- What are our disposal costs?

- Can this be recycled?
- Is recycling more affordable?
- How can we close the loop on recycling efforts?

Examples:

Choosing a destination with recycling infrastructure. This is a key decision that will make your work implementing a recycling program much easier. During the request for proposal process ask the recycling questions, tour the facility, and learn what is involved and what is possible. It is possible to set up a recycling system in a facility or city that currently doesn't have one, but it is much more time consuming. Find out if composting is available and what can be composted. Food waste is extremely heavy and will impact your waste hauling fees.

Additionally, make sure to include language in the contract requiring that recycling is actually accomplished, measured and reported. The contract should have "teeth" in it to make sure destinations comply, such as holding the final 10% of payment until the measurement figures are turned in.

Saving money on waste hauling charges. As show and event organizers know, you are charged for hauling away the waste from your event. While sometimes the first haul is free, the rest are charged at the local rate. During a comparison several years ago, one haul from Moscone Center was $1,200, Oregon Convention Center was $750 and the Georgia Dome was $35. While this charge fluctuates greatly, it is only going to increase in the future and it significantly impacts your bottom line. Check on the cost for **hauling away recyclable materials**. Most cities do not charge for this service.

Items that are donated to the local community are picked up by that organization and are not included in your **waste hauling charges**.

Using volunteers to maximize recycling efforts. Managing the waste stream can be complex for the participant in a hurry to dispose of an item, especially if there is a composting stream available. One way to significantly increase your recycling numbers is to use "green angels" stationed by the recycling stations to assist people with selecting the right bin. Statistics and experience show the impact. This should also be looked at as a sponsorship opportunity. Sponsors like to create a good image and sponsoring the green angels allows them to do just that. They can sponsor in cash you can use to purchase T-shirts and equipment for recycling efforts or in cash and by providing employees to serve as volunteers. It is amazing how many photos of these helpers in T-shirts (with a company logo) end up in the event publicity.

Other sources of staffing include your own attendees or student volunteers, local schools with ecology clubs, environmental groups and local master recyclers who would work for a donation to their organization.

Purchasing materials that are recyclable or compostable may save money. The key to the process is, of course, to have materials that are either recyclable or compostable if composting is available. Make sure the materials you purchase meet this criterion and save you money. The prices on many of these products have dropped dramatically, and they are more readily available with the increased demand. At the same time, the cost of oil- and petroleum-based products has gone up. If you have questions when purchasing the products, check with the venue or vendor that will be recycling the products.

Case studies:

Fairmont San Francisco Cuts Trash, Saves Money

As one of the first hotel chains to strategically brand their sustainable practices, Fairmont Hotels and Resorts operates a chainwide Eco-Meet Program that benefits thousands of meetings across the world by reducing impacts and saving money. The Fairmont San Francisco estimates it saved $10,000 per month in 2009 by improving property recycling and composting programs. The hotel cuts costs by diverting as much material as possible from landfill, estimating a typical 64% diversion rate. Even kitchen grease is captured for use as biofuel!

Canada Media Marketplace Gets Clever with Name Badges

For a small 300-person event name badges are not a huge cost. Perhaps $100 at most. But what if you could eliminate this cost and create a cool sponsorship idea? This is exactly what Canada Media Marketplace did. Canadian destinations participating in the event are always looking for interesting and unique ways to enhance their profile with travel writers invited to attend this event in hopes it might generate positive press for them. In 2009, Ontario Tourism had a brilliant idea: sponsor handmade name badges by Toronto-based designer James Fowler. What better reminder of their destination than a beautiful piece of art hanging on the neck of every attendee? To make the story even greener, badges were made from reclaimed container plastics and textile trimmings that would have otherwise been discarded. The name badges were a hit, and are still in use three years later, multiplying that $100 savings forward a year at a time!

SUMMARY

As you can see by the examples and case studies, reducing costs through green meeting practices is practical, easy, and essential to both your event budget and the environment. It is also fun, creative and forward-thinking. These ideas are just the start to what can be accomplished. With the commitment of your organization and the help of other passionate individuals within its structure, there is no limit. Remember to measure your success, show key stakeholders what you are saving by these programs. One green champion at a San Francisco hotel decided to take it upon himself to develop the recycling program when management wasn't really listening. He recently reported that they are listening now — the hotel is saving $5,000 a month in waste hauling fees. He is now looking for his next step.

The same goes for meeting managers. In 2008 through 2010, MeetGreen® clients avoided $3,937,993 in total costs by implementing sustainability measures. The return on investment in sustainable measures was 13.9.

SECTION IV

MEASURE

Now that you have lots of ideas of where cost savings might exist for your sustainable meeting, it's time to measure your impact. Measurement is one of the most important steps in being sustainable, but it is also often the most overlooked. We're getting better at showing environmental event metrics like waste, but determining cost savings is equally important. This is where you prove the business case for your sustainability effort and really hit home the financial value of your work to your organization.

Consider this: In many cities it is starting to pay to recycle. As landfill space fills up and manufacturing materials get scarcer, the cost to send materials to landfill is becoming more expensive than recycling in some American cities. For example, in Philadelphia, it costs $65 per ton to trash waste, and only 33 cents per ton to recycle! If your event produces 100 tons of trash and recycles half of it, you could save $3,000 in disposal fees by recycling. Imagine what you could avoid if you reduce and reuse as well as recycle! Similar situations exist in Minneapolis and San Francisco where trash taxes actually incentivize recycling, making it more financially attractive for venues, hotels and restaurants to minimize what is sent to landfill.

Once you have set an objective of saving money, measuring your cost savings is a simple four-step process:
- Set the baseline
- Select the indicators
- Affirm a target
- Communicate impact

In this section, we show you different ways to measure. How you chose to measure depends on your purpose. Do you want to show the difference between alternative decisions you could make? Do you want to show the short- and long-term impact of a decision? Do you want to show the overall costs and savings of your green meeting measures? Or do you want to compare funds invested in greening against sponsorship revenues? In the following sections, we will show what kinds of reports work best for different situations. These reports are:
- **Multi-Year Cost-Savings Model:** This shows the return on investment resulting from a green decision over time. It can show gross and net costs.
- **Single-Year Cost-Savings Budget:** This report communicates how your investment in different green actions balances across all event areas. It shows how multiple

actions compare within one event, to ensure your overall budget trades-off in a neutral way between items that cost more and cost less.
- **Sponsorship Model:** If you want to show what you're investing in green, and how you're offsetting it through financial sponsorships for a single event, this is the report for you.

Set the Baseline

To know where you're going, you need to know where you've been. That's why it is critical to establish your baseline for calculating cost savings. Ideally, this baseline should be set prior to your cost-saving measures being implemented. This will allow you to show maximum value for your actions. For example, if you start to implement green practices this year, you may want to select the previous year as your baseline for measuring the financial implications of these decisions. In each subsequent year you can then compare not only your savings from the previous year, but also the cumulative impact since your baseline was set.

> **APEX Glossary**
>
> **Baseline:** *A point of reference to enable comparisons. A baseline is a starting point for data that you use to show the impact of a decision. In the case of costs for event sustainability, the baseline is most likely a budget from a specific event at a point in time, or your department as a whole.*

This is an important point because the direct cost is usually only reduced in the first year, then it becomes "invisible" in subsequent years when the practice is continued. If you don't continue to compare to your baseline you may forget the financial justification for your decision and revert to a practice that costs you money.

To illustrate the point, consider the simple practice of eliminating bottled water. Opting to not provide bottled water reduces waste and saves energy, water, emissions and money. The baseline for your decision should be the last year you provided bottled water. Let's say you guaranteed 1,000 bottles of water per day for your three-day event last year. The cost for this was $7,500, which you would record as a gross cost savings in your first year of eliminating this item.

Cost Savings for a Single Year

Action	Budget savings	Budget overage
Produced a pocket-program instead of a full program	$10,000	-
Used 100% recycled content paper	-	$3,000
Developed online program scheduler	-	$10,000
Eliminated buses by selecting walkable hotels	$10,000	-
Eliminated water bottles	$7,500	-
Rented water bubblers	-	$5,000
TOTAL	$27,500	$18,000
NET SAVINGS (INDICATOR)	$9,500	

See page 52 for a full-size worksheet

Tip: To show the <u>cumulative impacts of a single decision over time</u> consider a Multi-Year Cost-Savings Model. These can show both gross and net impacts on your financial baseline.

For **Multi-Year Cost Savings**, a reporting line item in your "greening budget" might look like this:

	Baseline Year Cost	Year 1 Cost
Bottled water	$7,500	$0

Although you may not experience another direct cost reduction the year following this decision, it is important to estimate total costs avoided over multiple event cycles. Over 10 years, this decision may have an impact of over $50,000, so don't discount your impact!

	Baseline	Year 1	Year 2	Year 3	Year 4	Year 5	Year 6	Year 7
Cost bottled water	$7,500	$0	$0	$0	$0	$0	$0	$0
Gross cumulative savings		$7,500	$15,000	$22,500	$30,000	$37,500	$45,000	$52,500

Another consideration is whether or not you are measuring gross or net costs. Gross costs are impressive, but ultimately beg the question of what investment was required to generate them. In the water bottle illustration, for example, you should reduce the $7,500 gross bottle purchase cost by the rental cost of any water bubblers and adjust your indicator accordingly. This may reduce the net savings over baseline, but provides a more accurate sense of actual costs.

Consider the **Multi-Year Cost-Savings Model** we gave earlier.

Cost Savings for Multiple Years								
	Baseline	Year 1	Year 2	Year 3	Year 4	Year 5	Year 6	Year 7
Cost bottled water	$7,500	$0	$0	$0	$0	$0	$0	$0
Gross cumulative savings	$0	$7,500	$15,000	$22,500	$30,000	$37,500	$45000	$52,500
Gross cumulative cost of water bubblers	$0	$5,000	$10,000	$15,000	$20,000	$25,000	$30,000	$35,000
Net Saving	$0	$2,500	$5,000	$7,500	$10,000	$12,500	$15,000	$17,500

This kind of cost modeling can be helpful to evaluate the potential long- and short-term impacts of decisions you are able to make. It can help to solve what we call "light bulb" dilemmas. You know what we mean: You have to switch out a bulb and know the CFL is three times the cost of the regular old bulb your parents used. But you know it will last longer and use less energy in time. Where you're finding yourself weighing the pros and cons of costs and savings over time, multi-year models like this can help show the short- and long-term perspectives on your decisions.

For example, you may want to consider this kind of model for a practice that might require more than a few years to pay off, such as investing in reusable event signage. When you make the switch to reusable signs, they need to be more durable and often initially cost more than disposable alternatives. Consider the following example: Last year you purchased 60 one-time use easel signs for your education sessions for a cost of $50 each. This year you have the option to buy a reusable alternative, but the cost is twice as much as the disposable alternative. Based on the model shown in the chart, you would need to ensure two years of use to make back your investment, if considering gross amounts. Over multiple years, the savings could be significant, but remember to be reasonable in terms of how long you expect signs to last. The tendency of your event to rebrand is another consideration that might affect this kind of return on investment analysis in materials you reuse year to year.

	Baseline	Year 1	Year 2	Year 3	Year 4	Year 5
Cost of session signs	$3,000	$6,000	$0	$0	$0	$0
Gross saving	$0	-$3,000	$0	$3,000	$6,000	$9,000

Also, be mindful of "hidden" costs to maintain and ship the signs. This might affect your net costs, and push out the time required to secure a return on your investment. Don't forget that shipping can have a carbon footprint that impacts the environment, in addition to your pocketbook.

Cost Savings for Multiple Years

	Baseline	Year 1	Year 2	Year 3	Year 4	Year 5
Cost of session signs	$3,000	$6,000	$0	$0	$0	$0
Gross saving	$0	-$3,000	$0	$3,000	$6,000	$9,000
Cost of sign inserts	$0	$50	$50	$50	$50	$50
Cost of shipping	$0	$300	$500	$200	$450	$100
Cost of carbon offset	$0	$30	$50	$20	$45	$10
Net Saving	$0	-$3,380	-$600	$2,730	$5,455	$8,840

Although planners can use this modeling, it is likely even more important for suppliers to consider. Audiovisual companies, hotels, meeting venues and general service contractors all have to evaluate short- and long-term return on investment. Consider the following applications:

- Should you invest in recycled carpet and padding?
- Is it worth the utility savings to switch to water-conserving fixtures? Or install a solar panel array?
- How long will it take to pay off the cost of upgrading to LED lighting for staging and sets?

Many suppliers are being pressured to upgrade to greener products, which may cost more money in the short term. Long-term cost-saving scenarios can create a better understanding between suppliers and planners about what kind of commitment is needed over what timeframe to make investments worthwhile. For example, if a supplier can show it would take 3 years to recoup an investment in greener A/V equipment, such evidence may lend support to solidifying a longer-term agreement with a planner to provide services. This minimizes the risk to the supplier, while enabling the planner to secure a greener service at no increase in cost. This example also shows how measurement is not just a post-event process, but plays an important role in negotiation as well.

Select the Indicators

On the surface this step may seem easy. After all, we're trying to save money here! The natural indicator is therefore dollars. Scratching below the surface, however, you may need to establish some rules for how you measure dollars.

One of the first considerations ties back to the purpose of tracking the economic impacts of sustainable events. On one level you want to demonstrate costs saved or avoided. On another level there may be an opportunity to show revenues earned. You may choose to show both when demonstrating the financial impact of your sustainability decision. These options have subtly different indicators, which are calculated in different ways. Cost-savings budgets tend to show net costs or savings as an indicator. Sponsorship models use net revenue or expense as an indicator.

> **APEX Glossary**
>
> **Indicator:** *A data point that is used to help share information and make decisions. Common indicators used in sustainable events may be dollars, pounds of waste, miles travelled or gallons of water used.*

*Tip: Want to know how our overall bottom line for a single event stacks up? Try a **Single-Year Cost-Savings Budget**. This kind of budget allows you to look at multiple actions that drive the cost indicator.*

To demonstrate overall **cost savings in a single budget year** consider this format. This is particularly helpful to show how different green actions that cost more can be balanced with those actions that save money.

See page 52 for a full-size worksheet

Single-Year Cost-Savings Budget		
Action	**Budget savings**	**Budget overage**
Produced a pocket program instead of a full program	$10,000	-
Used 100% recycled content paper	-	$3,000
Developed online program scheduler	-	$10,000
Eliminated buses by selecting walkable hotels	$10,000	-
Eliminated water bottles	$7,500	-
Rented water bubblers	-	$5000
TOTAL	$27,500	$18,000
NET SAVINGS (INDICATOR)	$9,500	

*Tip: If you want to show your green expenses over sponsorship revenues, consider using a **Sponsorship Model** to show your cost savings.*

If you are adopting a **Sponsorship Model** for funding your sustainable practices to maximize even more savings by creating revenue opportunities, consider this format. This works particularly well if you are supporting special projects and programs to green your event.

Sponsorship Model		
Expense Item:		
Jute conference bag	$10,000	
Reusable water bottle	$7,500	
Recycling center signage	$2,000	
Shirts, training and appreciation for Event Green Team	$7,500	
Print/download stations	$10,000	
Certified organic food for breaks	$5,000	
Nonprofit exhibit pavilion	$10,000	
Carbon offset	$8,000	
Total		**$60,000**
Revenue Item:		
Green Exhibit Pavilion sponsor	$12,500	
Carbon offset sponsor	$10,000	
Recycling Center sponsor	$10,000	
CyberCafe sponsor	$10,000	
Wellness Break sponsor (2 @ $2,500)	$5,000	
Green event sponsorships (2 @ $10,000)	$20,000	
Total		**$67,500**
NET REVENUE (INDICATOR)		**$7,500**

See page 49 for a full-size worksheet

Whichever model you choose, it is important to stick with it. Strive to track cost and environmental data in a consistent way. Interpret the data using percentages, but never forget to document your raw data from year to year to ensure a strong basis for comparison.

Affirm a Target

Once you have set a baseline of budget information and are clear on what indicators you will include in your calculations, set a goal to achieve. Challenge yourself to see if you can reduce costs by a reasonable percentage of your baseline budget. Set a dollar value as a goal. Identify a sponsorship target. Estimate a minimum number of years you will commit to keep products in inventory as a way to increase life cycle and reduce long-term costs. Having a target in mind can be a key way to engage and motivate staff and vendors to achieve it. Don't overlook the power of publicizing your goal and giving others opportunities to share in the rewards of success. Allowing staff to share in a portion of costs saved can be a great incentive to work toward them.

> **APEX Glossary**
>
> **Target:** *An objective or goal you hope to achieve.*

Communicating Impact — and the Impact of Communicating!

There are many good reasons to measure. However, there are some cautions to be aware of before you decide how to communicate your cost savings.

On the positive side, you want to show how you and your team are adding specific value by protecting the planet AND being mindful of the financial bottom line. On the other hand, meeting budgets are already under scrutiny, so it is important to not compromise your available funds for creating successful meetings by communicating a message you didn't intend.

Some tips that can help you to communicate your cost-savings green measures include:
- Centralizing reporting
- Identifying your audiences and messages
- Being transparent

Centralize Reporting

Although different elements of your meeting may be managed by different individuals and different parties may be involved in procurement, it is important to establish one person to collect all the information related to the cost and benefit of "going green." Budgets are managed and decisions are made by different individuals, departments and facilities. They also take place at different times. One person needs to compile information across these multiple scopes and show the effect on your overall bottom line. This person is an important cog in the wheel of analyzing this information so the event team can effectively use it to make decisions. You may find, for example, that the cost savings of reducing hard copy communications frees up funds to invest in other green practices, such as buying organic food. Without your green budget coordinator, the managers of these different areas may never make a connection and may not realize how the costs avoided by going green can be reinvested in other areas of the event.

Make sure you outline clear rules of the road for collecting cost-saving data. This is particularly important for suppliers and planners who are responsible for tracking and compiling cost savings across multiple events or facilities. Different staff may be responsible for reporting data from certain aspects of your event or facility, so make sure you outline clear terms of reference for them, including any assumptions and instructions. Instructions may include clarifying how and by when you want data collected. Stipulate instructions for disclosing gross and net costs. Ensure that your food service coordinator tracks savings in the same way your meeting logistics, transportation and registration coordinators do.

Have you ensured that your vendors will be forthcoming with the savings realized? It is critical you have a conversation with your vendors upfront about your expectations of sharing the savings with you. Realize they may be reluctant to do so if they feel it will lower their bottom line or potential income from you. If you have contracts with a supplier, be sure to include a clause requiring them to disclose cost comparisons and an expected time line to receive the information. This issue is discussed in more detail in the negotiation section.

Identify Audiences and Messages

How, with whom and to what extent your cost-saving information is shared is highly individual. The first step is to determine who you will share information with. Is the information to be shared only with the event team or management? Will you be sharing this information with members, the board, media or other stakeholders? Will this information be included in your annual report? Answering the "who" questions first will enable you to determine to what extent and how the information will be shared.

Common audiences you may want to share information with include:
- Internal team
- Senior management
- Board
- Meeting attendees
- Members/customers
- Media

Carefully consider what information these audiences will be interested in, and the impact of sharing it. Your senior managers may be most interested in the overall savings. The board may be interested in these as well, in addition to how they can communicate the impact of actions that contribute to positive company image. Because these audiences have influence over your budget, it is important to show how funds saved can be reinvested in the experiences you create.

Meeting attendees do not typically receive information about cost savings from greening. There are benefits to including this audience, however. Savvy attendees will be able to see how your green practices are reducing or avoiding costs. If these actions are not supported with information about how you are adding value in other ways, attendees may question registration fees.

You may also want to share your information outside your company or association. The meetings industry needs your help in dispelling the myth that green meeting practices cost more money. Any information you're willing to share to show others how they too can benefit will be a win-win-win. Sharing the information will position you as a leader in the industry — your win. Others will be encouraged to engage in environmentally responsible practices — their win. The more of our industry greening their meetings, the better off the economy and environment are — our world's win.

Transparency

In virtually every instance it is important to be transparent about savings. It is also important to show the impact of these savings and how they are allowing you to reinvest in other parts of the event. Telling the whole story helps to reduce risks.

Itemizing costs saved and incurred through a cost-savings budget or sponsorship model can clearly demonstrate how reduced costs are being reinvested to expand and add value for attendees. This reduces the risk attendees may criticize you for cutting back on services, while keeping registration fees constant.

Similarly, sharing these budgets and models with senior management will show that you are leveraging more out of your event budgets, which is critical. This mitigates the risk your budgets may be cut where managers only see savings by being green.

One of the greatest barriers to fully integrating sustainability into event planning is that greening is often addressed in the last few months or weeks before an event, as a side project. Integrating the kinds of cost-saving analysis proposed in this book will allow you to approach event sustainability more strategically. You will be able to see the bigger picture of how green practices create costs and benefits that transect different event functions. This approach can challenge how we normally budget for events and plan for them. Transparency and centralized coordination of reporting is therefore critical to enable all stakeholders to understand how they affect and influence.

Promotional Benefits

Today, planning a sustainable event often earns you and/or your organization promotional benefits. This is especially true if you've produced cost-effective results by applying a creative approach to the event. Be sure as you're considering all of the financial impacts of your events and consider the promotional potential as well. Consider that the following opportunities are often positive additions to your bottom line:

- If you are quoted in or wrote an article for a magazine.
    - One way to calculate the worth of this type of coverage is to take the approximate space your quote or article takes up on the page and multiply it by the equivalent ad space costs (This is for a printed piece. Online press is certainly factored differently). For example: You were quoted throughout an article and the space your quotes amounted to was half a page. The average ad space cost for a half page is $5,500. Therefore, because you greened your event you received magazine coverage worth $5,500. I'm sure you've heard

the phrase "you can't buy that type of advertising because getting your name in and work recognized in a magazine is priceless."
- Speaking opportunities that should include a stipend or speaker fee.
    - Speaking engagements can also lead to meeting potential clients and more positive recognition for you and your organization.
- Blog post, tweet feeds and other social media should also be researched. Data is just being collected to attempt to quantify and qualify social media. Link backs also increase your search engine rankings, which helps to drive more traffic to your Web sites and social media sites.
- Awards and recognition programs may also have a financial return. For example, if a picture was taken of you or your team accepting the award and it was published, you are now back to reaping the rewards noted in the first bullet point.

The point is the free press and accolades are the frosting on the cake and should not be overlooked as having a substantial value to you and your organization. Enroll colleagues early in the process to develop a media strategy around the green initiatives. Too often, organizations think they must be 100% to even start telling the story. But what most people are most interested in is the transparent story about what worked and what was learned.

CONCLUSION

Money talks. Cost savings can create the incentive to plan green events, and provide new ideas and revenue streams that sustain the effort. Throughout this workbook we've provided steps, examples and tools to illustrate that what makes sustainability sense also makes business sense: The two are interconnected.

As demonstrated, the successful strategies for saving green by being green include:
- Thinking about sustainability as early in the planning process as possible.
- Being aware of how much time and support you have to implement your effort and prioritize what is most important.
- Understanding your supply chain and leveraging these relationships to reduce costs and add value.
- Measuring the net impact on your budget and the environment.

Ultimately, planning a green event is how you demonstrate smart business practices. Being able to demonstrate the value you bring in creating environmental, social and business benefits solidifies the important role you play in contributing to your organization's success.

SECTION VI

Worksheets

To help you apply the lessons learned in this book we encourage you to make use of the following blank templates.

Commitment Level Checklist 47

Sponsorship Model 49

Analysis of the Impact of Sustainable Options 50

Supply Chain Inventory 51

Cost Savings for a Single Year 52

Cost Savings for Multiple Years 53

Commitment Level Checklist

Use this form to inventory how committed your organization is to holding a sustainable event. Consider what strategies might help to increase support for sustainable practices.

1. How interested are the following in sustainability?	Very uninterested	Uninterested	Neutral	Interested	Very interested
Stockholders					
Senior Management					
Middle Management					
Employees					
Members (if applicable)					
Sponsors (if applicable)					
Vendors					
Me					
Others (if applicable)					

2. For those stakeholders who are interested in sustainability, why are they interested? What attracts them?

3. For those stakeholders not interested in sustainability, what makes them that way? What repels them?

Commitment Level Checklist

4. Is the organization:	Yes	No
Willing to spend extra time to be green?		
Willing to be green but not spend additional time?		
Willing to spend money to be as green as possible?		
Willing to be green, but only at no additional cost?		
Only willing to be green if it saves money?		
Interested in practices that reflect well on their image?		
Interested in practices that reduce risk?		
Concerned being green may reduce experience quality?		
Able to devote human resources to greening the event?		

5. Can any of the following be harnessed to help get commitment for your sustainable event?	Notes:
Company or event sustainability policy	
Attendee or sponsor feedback	
Employee support	
Vendor support / products / services	
Positive press coverage / presentation or award opportunities	
Demonstrated cost savings	
Standards / regulations affecting your event	
Risk factors (negative PR, additional costs)	
Other	

Sponsorship Model

List those expenses associated with sustainable decisions. Identify sponsorship options to offset any extra costs.

Expense Item:		

Total

Revenue Item:		

Total

NET REVENUE (INDICATOR)

Analysis of the Impact of Sustainable Options

For each action outline the impact in terms of costs, attendee experience, sponsorship, public relations and sustainability.

Action	Cost impact	Attendee impact	Sponsor impact	Promotional impact	Sustainability impact
Examples: Eliminating conference bags, local and organic food procurement	Indicate specific $ increases or decreases	Describe how the action will affect the event experience	Describe how sponsor benefit might be positively or negatively impacted	Describe the impact in terms of public relations and image	Describe specific environmental or social benefits in terms of energy, water, waste, pollution, community involvement

Supply Chain Inventory

This is a basic list of all items typically purchased for a conference. Using this spreadsheet during the planning and budgeting phase will help you make critical decisions to save both money and the environment whenever possible.

Item	Vendor	Sustainability Features / Criteria	Cost Implications
	Who is providing this product/service?	*What kind of environmental or social responsibility criteria does the product/service meet?*	*What are the financial savings or costs of this decision?*
Meeting rooms			
Sleeping rooms			
Airfare			
Ground transportation			
Airport transportation			
Shuttle transportation			
Speaker expenses			
Food and beverage			
Breaks			
Lunch			
Dinner/reception			
Audiovisual/production			
Internet connectivity			
Equipment rental			
General service contractor			
Electronic material production			
Printed materials, printed program, inserts			
Handouts or bag inserts			
Giveaway or promotional items			
Conference bag			
Name badges and supplies			
Pre-registration announcements			
Clerical expenses			
Temp staff or volunteers			
Telephone			
Online registration			
Postage and shipping			
Signage			

Total
(above or below budget)

Cost Savings for a Single Year

Action	Budget savings	Budget overage

TOTAL

NET SAVINGS (INDICATOR)

Cost Savings for Multiple Years

	Baseline	Year 1	Year 2	Year 3	Year 4	Year 5
NET SAVINGS						

SECTION VII

Checklists

Basic best practices are a good place to start if you're looking to reduce the environmental impact of your event and save money. It's always best to create your own list that works for you, your organization and the types of events you plan. The following checklists can be used as they are if you need something to send to your suppliers, or they may help you get started on your own customized best practices.

Accommodation Selection:
Rest Assured 55

Audiovisual and Production 57

Communications and Marketing 59

Destination Selection:
The First Step to a Sustainable Event........................... 61

Exhibition Production:
Working with a General Service Contractor 63

Exhibition Production:
What to Ask Exhibitors 65

Food and Beverage:
Making Fresh, Healthy, Sustainable Food Choices 67

Meeting Venue Selection:
Partners in a Sustainable Meeting 69

Transportation:
Minimizing the Impact of Moving People.................... 71

Accommodation Selection: Rest Assured

We are seeking to expand the reach of the sustainable event program by inviting all client events to join us in championing sustainable event practices. With this in mind, we would like you to consider the following when selecting accommodations for event participants. We also invite you to share your ideas and successes with us as we continuously refine our best practices.

Request that the hotel implement the following procedures and practices during the meeting at no additional cost:

- Provide a recycling program (recycling paper, plastic, glass, aluminum cans, cardboard and grease) for the entire hotel including sleeping rooms and meeting space.
- Provide clearly marked recycling containers in common areas, including the lobby, and in guest rooms unless the hotel sorts and recycles back of house.
- Instruct the housekeeping staff to shut blinds and turn down the heat/air conditioning and turn off lights during the day in rooms while attendees are gone.
- Implement a towel and sheet reuse program.
- Use energy-efficient lighting in all meeting and guest rooms.
- Instruct the housekeeping staff to not replace individually packaged consumable amenities daily unless they are gone. Use of soap and shampoo dispensers would be optimal. Participate in an amenity donation program or refill individual containers.
- Use glass or china (nondisposable) catering plates, cups and glasses.
- If food-and-beverage service is booked through the hotel, they will be expected to adhere to the food-and-beverage guidelines.
- If food-and-beverage events are not booked in hotel, the hotel is to offer locally grown, organic options in food-and-beverage outlets. Polystyrene is not to be used in any venue of the hotel including guest rooms.
- Use cleaning products that do not introduce toxins into the air.
- Use bottled water bearing a third-party verified eco-label.

Don't forget to measure your efforts

If possible, we encourage you to track your success. Ask the hotel venue to report on the weights or amounts of recyclables, compost and waste sent to the landfill. Also ask for product specifications or third-party certifications for any cleaning products and toilet papers. If possible, have them track the number of guests participating in the towel/sheet reuse program.

Helpful Tools and Resources
- MeetGreen® Hotel Survey
- MeetGreen® Hotel Contract Language
- MeetGreen® Hotel Measurement Checklist
- Green Seal Certified Hotels http://www.greenseal.org/FindGreenSealProductsandServices/HotelsandLodgingProperties.aspx
- Earth Check (formerly Green Globe) Certified Properties http://www.earthcheck.org/en-us/certification/default.aspx
- Green Key Eco-Rating Program http://www.greenkeyglobal.com/hotellistall.asp
- Sustainable Travel International http://www.sustainabletravelinternational.org/green/sti_membership/search

---

Fast Facts:

Saving water saves money. *Towel and sheet reuse programs save a typical 150-room hotel 6,000 gallons of water and 40 gallons of detergent per month, which translates directly into utility savings. (Source: Sustainable Lodging Program, 2004). If a hotel indicates to you they don't provide linen reuse, ask them why they wouldn't want to save money!*

A bright idea to save money. *The Fairmont Royal York has saved $51,000 per year by switching from incandescent to fluorescent lights. In addition, the Hyatt Maui estimates new energy-efficient guest room thermostats have saved $64 per room, or more than $50,000 annually. (Data sourced from John Rosenthal, "Why Hotels Go Green," published in National Geographic Traveler, Jan/Feb 2004 Issue).*

Sustaining the Triple Bottom Lines. *Through its Sustainability Indicator Reporting program that tracks both energy and water conservation measures Scandic Hotels estimates it has saved EUR 18 million between 1996–2000. That's over $27.7 million USD! (Scandic Hotels, 2008).*

Audiovisual and Production

We are seeking to expand the reach of the sustainable event program by inviting all client events to join us in championing sustainable event practices. With this in mind, we would like you to consider the following when selecting audiovisual and production providers for events. We also invite you to share your ideas and successes with us as we continuously refine our best practices.

Consider implementing the following sustainable practices when designing the audiovisual and production components of your event:

- Include environmental requests in the RFP and contracts for the audiovisual and staging company.
- Scenic and stage design:
  - Source products locally to eliminate or reduce the need for harmful emissions.
  - Use Forest Stewardship Certified (FSC) or Scientific Certification Systems (SCS) certified wood.
  - Incorporate recycled materials such as old tires, oil drums, aluminum cans, etc. into the set design and then dispose of them properly.
  - Use water-based instead of solvent–based paints to minimize toxic emissions. Water-soluble latex paints typically contain fewer volatile organic compounds.
  - Reuse and donate material after the show.
  - Avoid toxic materials. Certain building materials should be avoided to the greatest extent possible, including PVC materials containing phthalate plasticizers, materials containing brominated flame retardants, and arsenic- or chromium-containing, preservative-treated wood.
  - Design for disassembly. All stage and infrastructure should be designed and constructed to facilitate easy deconstruction. This might include: a) designing to standard dimensions (e.g., 4' x 8') so that sheet goods can be salvaged full size; b) using screws and bolts for fabrication as opposed to adhesives and nail guns; and c) engaging a deconstruction contractor at the outset.
- Audiovisual and video providers:
  - Use the most efficient projector based on audience requirements, venue limitations and audience needs.
  - Participate in a lamp recycling program for all projector bulbs and ballasts.

- Sound providers:
  - Use an efficient, lightweight, cooler "Switch Mode Power Supply" to drive the sound system.
  - Use a compact, high-efficiency speaker system.
- Lighting providers:
  - Integrate LED lights.
  - Use the most efficient lighting based on audience requirements, venue limitations and audience needs.
  - Participate in a lamp recycling program for all expended bulbs and ballasts.

Don't forget to measure your efforts

If possible, we also encourage you to track your success. This area has the capacity for a significant energy savings. Ask your vendors to calculate the energy savings.

Fast Facts:

Red light, yellow light, green light — go! *Planners will most likely encounter cost differences in lighting when it comes to A/V production. In general, planners can expect an increase of 50–150% in cost where LEDs are used. However, these increases should be compared with the savings associated with using LEDSs. These savings can include reduced need for dimmers and color gel filters, which are often charged out per unit, as well as savings from using smaller, more compact equipment and less power. Powering an LED lighting system is 75% cheaper than a conventional system (Hollywood Lighting, 2008).*

MeetGreen®
Connect. Sustain. Thrive.

Communications and Marketing

We are seeking to expand the reach of the sustainable event program by inviting all client events to join us in championing sustainable event practices. With this in mind, we would like you to consider the following when marketing and communicating about your event. We also invite you to share your ideas and successes with us as we continuously refine our best practices.

Use online methods of communication
With today's technology, using online methods of communication wherever possible and appropriate works toward a goal of paperless meetings. This includes taking advantage of:
- Electronic ticketing and reservation systems
- Online registration
- Electronic rooming lists, room layouts and banquet event orders
- Online program/agenda
- Online exhibitor kits
- Digital signage
- Downloadable speaker presentations and handouts
- Electronic event evaluations

Consider signage
When using signage, you should consider the following practices:
- Limit the number of signs necessary for events.
- Reduce use of disposable signage by designing signs for reuse. By not including the date or location, signage may be available for use in subsequent years or by other events, which will have a very favorable impact on your budget.
- If signage is necessary, it should be made from recycled and recyclable or biodegradable materials.
- Electronic signage should be used whenever possible.

Minimize printing or make responsible choices
- Use of printed materials will be avoided as a priority.
- If printing is required, printers will be requested to use:
  - Post-consumer recycled content paper (minimum 30%) that is unbleached or bleached without chlorine
  - Vegetable-based inks
  - Printed double-sided

Share our sustainable story

MeetGreen® has received a lot of publicity about the sustainable practices we incorporate, and that has put MeetGreen® in a leadership position within this industry. It is important to share information about our sustainable meeting story through our Web site and press releases. Each of the following key stakeholders should to be included in the communications plan:
- Senior management
- Employees
- Event attendees
- Sponsors
- Vendors
- Exhibitors
- Press

Don't forget to measure your efforts

Many of these sustainable practices can be measured environmentally, economically, and in media attention. You should provide cost accounting for reducing printing or switching to greener paper choices. In addition, provide a report of environmental savings using the Neenah Paper Calculator when greener paper options are chosen.

Helpful Tool
- Environmental Paper Network Paper Calculator http://www.papercalculator.org/

Fast Facts:

Green meetings, positive public relations. *Promotional spin-offs of the event greening practices adopted at the 2004 USA national political conventions included 90 published articles, 25 public presentation opportunities, 4 television appearances and 3 radio interviews. (Coalition for Environmentally Responsible Conventions Greening the US 2004 Democratic and Republication Conventions, 2004).*

Destination Selection:
The First Step to a Sustainable Event

We are seeking to expand the reach of the sustainable event program by inviting all client events to join us in championing sustainable event practices. With this in mind, we would like you to consider the following when selecting your event destination. We also invite you to share your ideas and successes with us as we continuously refine our best practices.

When choosing a destination for your meeting, look for a city that provides:

- **A meeting venue** able to provide recycling, practice energy efficiency and water conservation, and demonstrate environmentally preferable purchasing of cleaners, paper products and catering supplies. Give preference to a meeting venue certified for both environmental construction and operating practices, such as LEED, BOMA, ISO 14000/14001, BS8901 or another recognized and credible indicator of environmentally responsible performance.
- Host **hotels** with established environmental practices for energy efficiency and water conservation. A recognized certification such as Green Seal, Green Key, or Earth Check (Green Globe) would be ideal. Hotels should be within walking distance or convenient transit access of the meeting venue.
- Sustainable **transportation** services. Important features would be:
  - Available public transit
  - High-occupancy shuttling/transit options between the airport and meeting venues
  - Availability and use of alternative fuel or hybrid taxis or buses
  - Carpooling or ride-sharing programs
- **Caterers or food-and-beverage** services that provide local, organic and vegetarian options and use china and linen service.
- **Municipal programs** that support sustainability, specifically recycling, composting and public transit programs.

Helpful Tools and Resources

- Best Places to Meet Green. Listing of cities and a calculator to help you determine which destination has the least amount of carbon emissions for your participants. http://www.bestplacestomeetgreen.com/
- International Association of Conference Centres, Leaders in Environmental Responsibility http://www.iacconline.org/education/index.cfm?fuseaction=environmental

---

Fast Facts:

Green destinations in demand. *According to IMEX, 84% of meeting and incentive planners would deliberately avoid a destination with a poor environmental record (2008).*

Green from the ground up. *Choosing a sustainable destination can make the process of planning a green meeting a whole lot easier. A city with a convenient transit system and venues and hotels within walking distance can reduce shuttling costs and contribute to attendee health. The availability of municipal recycling and composting programs also often means these services can be provided for the event at no additional cost.*

MeetGreen®
Connect. Sustain. Thrive.

Exhibition Production:
Working with a General Service Contractor

We are seeking to expand the reach of the sustainable event program by inviting all client events to join us in championing sustainable event practices. With this in mind, we would like you to consider the following when selecting a general service contractor for your event. We also invite you to share your ideas and successes with us as we continuously refine our best practices.

Request that the general service contractor implement the following procedures and practices during the exhibit:

- Reduce the lights, power and heating/air-conditioning during move-in and move-out times in the exhibit hall.
- Provide online exhibitor kits/service.
- Use precut, to length, non-vinyl tabletops, wooden tables and biodegradable trash can liners.
- Use signage products made of environmentally responsible, recyclable components with applied and removable water-based graphics.
- Use reusable signage and graphics in registration counter/kiosks.
- Use show furniture and shelves that are made of renewable resources or certified forest products and that do not contain tropical hardwoods or endangered wood species.
- Use carpet made from recycled materials that are fully recyclable.
- Use natural gas forklifts and handcarts to move exhibitor freight in and out of the show to assist in the air quality.
- Reuse shipping and packing materials. Make biodegradable shipping and packing materials available to exhibitors and show management.
- Partner with a local contractor to manage and use local labor.
- Minimize transportation to and from the show site. Use biodiesel-fueled or alternative fuel trucks.
- Provide and manage a donation area for exhibitors to collect donated items.
- Participate in the venue recycling program.

Don't forget to measure your efforts
If possible, we also encourage you to track your success! Ask if the general service contractor can provide information on the environmental specifications of carpet, signage, cleaning products and tabletops a minimum of 30 days prior to the event.

Helpful Tool
- Carpet recycling calculator http://www.carpetrecovery.org/ for the general service contractor

---

Fast Facts:

The Green Market Revolution. *Having a hard time getting your general service contractor on board with your green exhibit practices? Try sharing the following information with them about the business case for greener exhibits and tradeshows:*

In many cities, such as London, the convention center will charge the decorator and meeting host extra for any materials not properly recycled.

The United States Environmental Protection Agency and the European meeting community are in the process of certifying trade shows and events for their environmental performance. Although not presently regulated, exhibitions are becoming subject to environmental guidelines.

Exhibition Production:
What to Ask Exhibitors

We are seeking to expand the reach of the sustainable event program by inviting all client events to join us in championing sustainable event practices. With this in mind, we would like you to consider providing the following guidelines to exhibitors at your event. We also invite you to share your ideas and successes with us as we continuously refine our best practices.

Ask exhibitors to implement the following procedures and practices during the trade show:

- Participate in the facility's recycling efforts by ensuring they recycle cardboard, freight boxes, plastic wrappings and other recyclable items during move-in and move-out.
- Make a conscious effort to minimize packing materials. Whenever possible, use environmentally responsible packing materials that are reusable, recyclable or biodegradable.
- Avoid large quantities of collateral and offer to send information upon request. Avoid dated material and use electronic methods.
- Print materials and signage using soy/vegetable-based ink and post-consumer, recycled products (minimum 30%).
- Provide promotional items made of recycled, responsibly grown natural fiber, and nontoxic and biodegradable materials. Ensure items are useful, not merely promotional in nature. Any food (candy, etc.) should be sustainably grown, processed and packaged. Giveaways with some imagination could also be electronic:
    - Free registration and free number of songs for iTunes
    - Free online subscriptions
    - Free Internet access
    - Free satellite TV
    - Free satellite radio
- Do not provide gift items made from endangered or threatened species. Consider gifts made locally or by indigenous people.
- Design booths and displays using environmentally responsible materials and energy-efficient lighting if applicable.
- Use local staff in the booth if possible.
- Minimize transportation to and from the show site. Use biodiesel or alternative fuel shipping methods.

- Inform and train staff about the environmentally responsible practices to be implemented during the show.
- Participate in the exhibit donation program by providing any materials that are eligible for donation.

Don't forget to measure your efforts

If possible, we also encourage you to track your success. Ask exhibitors about their sustainability efforts. You may even want to start a "Green Booth" awards program so they can receive recognition for their work.

Fast Facts:

Sustainability Sponsorship. *With a little creativity sustainable meeting practices can open up new sponsorship and exhibitor opportunities that contribute to the show budget and enhance attendee satisfaction. This can include creating a sustainability pavilion at a trade show or exhibit, featuring members, sponsors and products that are environmentally and socially responsible. Consider scheduling seminars and demonstrations at the pavilion to drive attendee participation.*

MeetGreen®
Connect. Sustain. Thrive.

Food and Beverage:
Making Fresh, Healthy, Sustainable Food Choices

We are seeking to expand the reach of the sustainable event program by inviting all client events to join us in championing sustainable event practices. With this in mind, we would like you to consider the following when selecting caterers for your event. We also invite you to share your ideas and successes with us as we continuously refine our best practices.

Consider implementing the following sustainable food-and-beverage practices for your event:

- Provide china and linen service, or if this is not possible, use biodegradable serviceware. Avoid polystyrene and #6 plastics if at all possible.
- Serve juice, water, ice tea and hot beverages in pitchers, urns or coolers, not individual containers or bottles.
- Serve condiments such as jam, jelly, sauces, sugar and cream in bulk (exception: serve sugar substitutes in individual servings).
- Do not pre-fill water glasses at a banquet meal.
- Donate any leftover unserved food to a local food bank.
- Use cloth napkins whenever possible. Use coasters instead of cocktail napkins. If paper napkins are necessary, use ones that contain post-consumer recycled paper.
- Use reusable, edible or living decorations rather than disposable ones.
- Use fair-trade, shade-grown coffee.
- Purchase any seafood according to the "Good" or "Best Alternative" choices under a sustainable fisheries program in your area (see resources).
- Compost prep food, table scraps and compostable serviceware.
- Try to maximize local and certified organic food in your menus. The definition of local food is within a 100-mile radius of your event.
- Request that the caterer use environmentally responsible cleaning products for kitchens, if they do not already do so.

Don't forget to measure your efforts

If possible, we also encourage you to track your success. Ask if the caterer can report how much material you compost, recycle and send to a landfill from your event (by weight). Also ask if they can let you know how much local and organic food they purchase, again by weight. We also encourage you to report how much food is donated from your event, if applicable.

Helpful Tools and Resources
- Monterey Bay Seafood Watch http://www.mbayaq.org/cr/SeafoodWatch.asp
- Seafood Choices Alliances links http://www.seafoodchoices.com/resources/links.php#organicresources
- Feeding America (North America food bank locator) http://feedingamerica.org/foodbank-results.aspx
- World Job and Food Bank (international food bank locator) http://www.wjfb.org/projects_category.htm#Food%20Banks
- US Bill Emerson Good Samaritan Food Donation Act of 1996 http://feedingamerica.org/partners/product-partners/protecting-our-partners.aspx

---

Fast Facts:

Sustainable menus can be cost effective. *Sometimes providing local-organic menus is a balancing act: look for cost savings that will help you invest in sustainable options. Caterers report saving up to 50–62% by providing condiments in bulk (MeetGreen, 2007). In 2006, the Vancouver Trade and Convention Centre provided a "from scratch" menu using only fresh, unpackaged ingredients to the World Urban Forum 3, resulting in 5% savings on produce costs (The Globe Foundation).*

Save your cup, save the planet. *By reusing a mug or bottle, IDF attendees can annually save 427 trees, enough energy to power three homes and 6,600 kg of solid waste. That's the weight of 4 cars. In 2007, MeetGreen saved a caterer $2,700 by switching from black plastic serviceware to a biodegradable alternative.*

Organic menus at nonorganic prices. *The United States Green Building Council and Unitarian Universalist Association successfully stipulate in contracts that a minimum of 25% of food and beverage will be sourced sustainably at no additional cost. This means organic food sourced within 100 miles of the meeting facility (MeetGreen, 2008).*

MeetGreen®

Connect. Sustain. Thrive.

Meeting Venue Selection:
Partners in a Sustainable Meeting

We are seeking to expand the reach of the sustainable event program by inviting all client events to join us in championing sustainable event practices. With this in mind, we would like you to consider the following when selecting a venue for your event. We also invite you to share your ideas and successes with us as we continuously refine our best practices.

Request that the meeting venue implement the following procedures and practices during the meeting:

- Minimize energy use by reducing the lights, power and heat/air-conditioning during move-in and move-out times in the exhibit hall and turning off lights in meeting rooms when not in use.
- Purchase green or renewable energy (solar, wind, tidal).
- Provide collection bins, facilities, staffing and training necessary to recycle all glass containers, aluminum and steel cans, plastic bottles, table coverings, pallets, paper (newspaper, cardboard and other office paper) and grease.
- Conserve natural resources by purchasing and providing all paper bathroom supplies with minimum 35% post-consumer recycled content paper.
- Minimize pollution and human exposure to toxic compounds by using environmentally responsible cleaning products bearing a third-party verified eco-label for carpets, floors, kitchens and bathrooms.
- Minimize air pollution by cleaning parking lots, sidewalks and driveways without the use of two-cycle combustion engines.
- If the meeting venue is providing food-and-beverage service, they will be expected to adhere to the food-and-beverage guidelines.

Don't forget to measure your efforts

If possible, we encourage you to track your success, Ask the meeting venue to report on the weights or amounts of recyclables, compost and waste sent to the landfill. Also ask for product specifications or third-party certifications for any cleaning products and toilet papers. If renewable energy was purchased, ask for proof for your records.

Helpful Tools and Resources

- International Association of Conference Centres, Leaders in Environmental Responsibility http://www.iacconline.org/education/index.cfm?fuseaction=environmental

---

Fast Facts:

Cost reduced through composting? *Food waste is typically the heaviest waste stream from an event. Many convention facilities are able to save money by composting where they can separate out heavier compostable material like food waste because it reduces the weight of trash hauled. Ask your convention facility how they handle waste and are charged for it. Cost savings may be possible.*

It pays to recycle. *Convention facilities and hotels are finding cost savings by diverting their waste from the landfill. This includes the city of San Francisco where it is more expensive to trash it than recycle it! Airports are also proving the benefits of recycling — saving an average of $100,000 USD per year by instituting recycling (National Resources Defense Council, 2006).*

Transportation:
Minimizing the Impact of Moving People

We are seeking to expand the reach of the sustainable event program by inviting all client events to join us in championing sustainable event practices. With this in mind, we would like you to consider the following when selecting transportation providers for your event. We also invite you to share your ideas and successes with us as we continuously refine our best practices.

The first step is to think about air transportation. Selecting a destination that is close and convenient for your attendees is often the best thing you can do to reduce the transportation footprint. Once you have considered how far attendees need to travel to your event, think about how you will transport them around the destination. Reduce shuttling where acceptable and appropriate to curb fuel use and greenhouse gas emissions. Review the meeting or event area to see which hotels, restaurants and attractions are within walking distance. While choosing the best location is always the goal, ground transportation is sometimes necessary due to distance, climate or security reasons.

Where ground transportation is necessary, strive to:
- Plan efficient routes and schedule shuttles during peak hours.
- Hire shuttle bus providers that operate greener fleets. This means operators may:
  - Use new, clean engine technologies and ultra-low-sulphur diesel. This typically means sourcing buses that are less than 3 years old.
  - Adopt hybrid engine technology.
  - Use biodiesel (B20 grade). This is a good way to allow older fleets to be more sustainable and only requires use of a new filter.
  - Adopt environmentally responsible maintenance procedures:
- Recycle used oil, batteries, antifreeze and tires.
- Minimize idling and the use of air conditioning especially when no passengers are in the vehicle.

Don't forget to measure your efforts!
In the case of transportation, tracking your success will also help you in future planning. Ask the transportation company to provide ridership reports to help track delegate use of the shuttles. Record how many transit passes were provided (if applicable). Ask attendees on evaluations if they walked between venues or used transit.

But what about carbon offsets?

A carbon offset is a project that is implemented to reduce the level of greenhouse gases in the atmosphere. Projects may include tree planting, renewable energy or energy efficiency investments. While offsets do allow meeting attendees and staff to be accountable for those emissions they can't avoid, offsets do not reduce the actual emissions associated with these activities. Instead of focusing on providing carbon offsetting, you can take steps to reduce emissions and the carbon footprint of meetings through diverse and proactive measures.

Fast Facts:

A walkable conference neighborhood makes a big difference! *Choosing hotels, venues and off-sites that are close to each other can reduce or eliminate the need to provide shuttles. Doing this at the 2002 Forest Leadership Forum saved $30,000–$40,000 for the three-day conference. (Meeting Strategies Worldwide, 2002).*

Get on the bus! *Consider comparing the cost of shuttling versus providing transit passes, if this is acceptable to the attendees. Better yet, ask the convention and visitor bureau to sponsor transit passes for your attendees as a way to get them to explore the city.*

Sponsor a walking challenge. *Consider asking a sponsor to provide pedometers to attendees. This can cut the cost and need for shuttles, earn new sponsorship dollars and engage attendees in getting active.*

One less pair of shoes. *If just one passenger per each flight in the world this year packed 1 pound less of luggage, they would save enough fuel to fly a Boeing 737 around the world 474 times. That's a lot of kerosene, and a lot of money! (Delta Sky Magazine, April 2008)*

LINKS/RESOURCES

Sustainable Event Standards
- APEX/ASTM Environmentally Sustainable Meeting Standards: http://www.conventionindustry.org/StandardsPractices/GreenMeetings/APEXASTM.aspx
- British Standard 8901: http://www.bsigroup.co.uk/en/Assessment-and-Certification-services/Management-systems/Standards-and-Schemes/BS-8901/
- Canadian Standards Association Z2010: http://shop.csa.ca/en/canada/quality-management-systems/z2010-2010/invt/27032182010/
- EcoLogo CCD-095 Events: http://www.ecologo.org/en/seeourcriteria/details.asp?ccd_id=320
- Global Reporting Initiative Event Sector Supplement: http://www.globalreporting.org/ReportingFramework/SectorSupplements/Events/
- ISO 20121: http://www.iso.org/iso/iso_catalogue/catalogue_tc/catalogue_detail.htm?csnumber=54552

Environmental Grants
- Australian Government Grants: http://australia.gov.au/topics/environment-and-natural-resources/environment-grants
- EcoAction Canada: http://www.ecoaction.gc.ca/grantsrebates-subventionsremises/organizations-organisations-eng.cfm
- European Commission Contracts and Grants: http://ec.europa.eu/contracts_grants/index_en.htm
- Natural Resources Canada: http://oee.nrcan.gc.ca/corporate/incentives.cfm
- U.S. federal grants: http://www.grants.gov/

Case Studies
- MeetGreen® event case studies, including Oracle OpenWorld, Business for Social Responsibility, Unitarian Universalist Association General Assembly and Canada Media Marketplace: http://meetgreen.com/resources/casestudies
- London 2012 Olympic and Paralympic Games Sustainability: http://www.london2012.com/making-it-happen/sustainability/index.php
- Vancouver 2010 Olympic and Paralympic Winter Games Sustainability Report: http://www.2010legaciesnow.com/vanoc_sustainability/

Products and Services
- GoGoGreenWorld: http://www.gogogreenworld.com/
- GoToMeeting: http://www.gotomeeting.com/
- Nexus Collections Search for a Sustainable Conference Bag: http://www.nexuscollections.com/environment.php?article=10
- Skype: http://www.skype.com/intl/en-us/home
- The Green Meeting Industry Council is an excellent source of information about suppliers of sustainable event products and services. Please refer to www.greenmeetings.info for further information.

Free Tools
- Best Places to MeetGreen® Destination Selection Tool: http://bestplacestomeetgreen.com/
- The Carbon Fund Calculator: http://www.carbonfund.org/Calculators/
- Carpet America Recovery Effort: http://www.carpetrecovery.org/
- The Climate Trust Carbon Calculator: http://www.climatetrust.org/content/calculators/Event_Calculator.pdf
- Environmental Defense Fund Paper Calculator: http://www.edf.org/papercalculator/
- Find a Food Bank: http://feedingamerica.org/default.aspx
- Local Foods Wheel: http://www.localfoodswheel.com/
- Seafood Watch: http://www.montereybayaquarium.org/cr/seafoodwatch.aspx
- Seasonal Ingredient Map: http://www.epicurious.com/articlesguides/seasonal-cooking/farmtotable/seasonalingredientmap
- State of Victoria (Australia) Event Calculator: http://www.epa.vic.gov.au/ecologicalfootprint/calculators/event/introduction.asp
- U.S. EPA Waste Calculators: http://www.epa.gov/climatechange/wycd/waste/tools.html

Laws and Regulations
- Bill Emerson Food Donation Act http://www.usda.gov/news/pubs/gleaning/appc.htm

Associations
- Green Meeting Industry Council: http://www.greenmeetings.info/

[Inclusion of resources in this section does not imply an endorsement of products or services by MeetGreen® and *we make no claims, warranties, or other representations concerning the accuracy, completeness, or utility of the information provided*.]

GLOSSARY

Note: Events-related glossary items were used with permission and sourced from APEX definitions.

accessibility requirements: Any regulations pertaining to making facilities accessible to disabled persons. For example, ramps for wheelchair access.

air quality monitoring: Any monitoring undertaken by a facility or third-party organization that reviews air quality.

alternative fuels: Alternative fuels encompass a wide range of fuel types including biofuels derived from corn, soy and recycled cooking oils, ethanol blended fuel, biodiesel, bioalcohol (methanol, ethanol, butanol), chemically stored electricity (batteries and fuel cells), hydrogen, nonfossil methane, nonfossil natural gas, vegetable oil and other biomass sources.

APEX: An acronym for Accepted Practices Exchange. APEX is an initiative of the Convention Industry Council that is bringing together all stakeholders in the development and implementation of industrywide accepted practices to create and enhance efficiencies throughout the meetings, conventions and exhibitions industry.

APEX Green Meeting & Events Guidelines:
http://www.conventionindustry.org/StandardsPractices/GreenMeetings.aspx

aqueous inks: Inks which can be dissolved by water instead of solvents.

attendee: See *participant*.

audiovisual: Also "A/V". Equipment, materials, and teaching aids used in sound and visual presentations, such as video projection, monitors, sound equipment, etc.

audit: 1) A methodical examination and review of records pertaining to an event. For instance, an independent verification of attendance figures submitted by an exhibition's producers. 2) An unbiased examination and evaluation of the financial statements of an organization. It can be done internally (by employees of the organization) or externally (by an outside firm).

bid: A proposal submitted by a convention and visitors bureau and/or hotel(s) or other suppliers to an event organizer that includes detailed specifications (such as dates, rates, concessions, etc.).

biodegradable: Capable of being broken down by natural processes, such as bacterial action.

biodiesel: A clean-burning, alternative fuel derived from animal fats or vegetable oil that can be used in diesel-burning engines. It does not contain petroleum products, but may be blended with petroleum-based diesel.

branded materials: Any materials that include the host organization and/or event name and logo (if available).

break: Short interval between sessions at which time coffee, tea and/or other refreshments are served. See also *refreshment break*.

break-even point: The point at which revenues are equal to expenses.

BS 8901: (BS 8901 stands for British Standard 8901). This standard is designed to help create management processes and practices (Event Management System or EMS) to support sustainability in meetings and events. The key requirements for BS8901 are: sustainability policy; issue identification and evaluation; stakeholder identification and engagement; objectives, targets and plans; performance against principles of sustainable development; operational controls; competence and training; supply chain management; communication; monitoring and measurement; corrective and preventive action; management system audits; and management review. More information and details can be found at: http://www.bsigroup.co.uk/en/Assessment-and-Certification-services/Management-systems/Standards-and-Schemes/BS-8901/

budget: A statement of estimated revenues and expenditures for a specified period of time, divided into subject categories and arranged by principal areas of revenue and expense.

budget philosophy: Financial goal of the event (break even, profit or lose money).

carbon dioxide (CO_2): A heavy, colorless gas that does not support combustion. Made of one carbon atom and two oxygen atoms, it is formed especially in animal respiration and in the decay or combustion of animal and vegetable matter. It is absorbed by plants in photosynthesis and is an atmospheric greenhouse gas.

carbon footprint: A measure of the impact human activities have on the environment in terms of the amount of greenhouse gases produced, measured in units of carbon dioxide.

carbon neutral: Carbon neutral is the point at which enough carbon is offset or sequestered to cover a specific amount of carbon generated by a manufacturing process, transportation method, product usage, building or individual.

carbon offset: A way of counteracting the carbon emitted when the use of fossil fuel causes greenhouse gas emissions. Offsets commonly involve investing in projects such as renewable energy, tree planting and energy-efficient projects.

citywide event: An event that requires the use of a convention center or event complex, as well as multiple hotels in the host city.

climate neutral: Products or services that reduce and offset the greenhouse gases generated at each stage of their life cycle on a cradle-to-cradle basis: the sourcing of their materials, their manufacturing or production, their distribution, use, and ultimate end-of-life disposition.

commercial composting: Commercial composting may include compost hauling or on-site composting facilities at businesses. Select the option that most closely matches the availability of commercial composting at the location of your event.

commercial recycling: Commercial recycling refers to recycling program and hauling that are available to businesses, as opposed to residential program. Select the option that most closely matches the availability of commercial recycling at the location of your event.

commission: A payment made to an individual or organization for bringing business to another individual or organization.

community projects: Community projects include any projects that give back directly to the community in the location where the event is being hosted. These can include one-time volunteer projects or legacy projects, which have a longer-term impact on the community. Legacy projects can be things such as establishing educational programs, raising money for a local charity, helping to build low-income housing, etc.

compost: A mixture of humus-rich, decomposed vegetable matter used as a fertilizer or soil enrichment.

composting: Composting is the result of a complex feeding pattern whereby aerobic microbes (bacteria and fungi that thrive on oxygen) feed on organic waste and break it down into a nutritious soil amendment. This can be done on a small scale in the home or on a larger scale for business and entire cities.

concessions: 1) Merchandise or refreshments sold on-site to individuals in conjunction with an event. 2) Contractual agreement wherein one party provides something of value to the other party in exchange for something else, pending certain conditions.

conference: 1) Participatory meeting designed for discussion, fact-finding, problem-solving and consultation. 2) An event used by any organization to meet and exchange views, convey a message, open a debate or give publicity to some area of opinion on a specific issue. No tradition, continuity or timing is required to convene a conference. Conferences are usually of short duration with specific objectives and are generally on a smaller scale than congresses or conventions.

conference center: A facility that provides a dedicated environment for events, especially small events. May be certified by the International Association of Conference Centers.

conference officer/organizer: Title generally conferred upon the chief administrator of the entire event.

congress: 1) The regular coming together of large groups of individuals, generally to discuss a particular subject. A congress will often last several days and have several simultaneous sessions. The length of time between congresses is usually annual, although some are on a less-frequent basis. Most international or world congresses are the latter type; national congresses are more frequently held annually. 2) European term for convention.

consumer show: Exhibition that is open to the public, usually requiring an entrance fee.

convention: Gathering of delegates, representatives, and members of a membership or industry organization convened for a common purpose. Common features include educational sessions, committee meetings, social functions, and meetings to conduct the governance business of the organization. Conventions are typically recurring events with specific, established timing. See also *meeting, exhibition, trade show, consumer show.*

convention center: Facility whose purpose it is to host trade shows, public shows, conventions, and other large functions and that combines exhibition space with a substantial number of smaller meeting and event spaces. A convention center may be purpose-built or converted and municipally or privately owned. See also *facility*.

corporate social responsibility (CSR): A form of corporate self-regulation whereby a business monitors and ensures its adherence to law, ethical standards and international norms.

damage clause: Part of a contract dealing with procedures, penalties and rights of the party causing damages.

decorator: An individual or company providing installation and dismantle and booth/stand and hall dressing services for a trade show and/or its exhibitors. Decorator services may be provided by carpenters, sign painters or others depending upon union jurisdiction. The term applies to both contractor and skilled craftsperson. See *general service contractor*.

direct spending: All expenditures associated with an event that flow into the host destination's local economy. Direct spending includes attendee spending, exhibitor spending and event organizer spending.

diversion rate: The percentage of waste materials diverted from traditional disposal such as landfilling or incineration to be recycled, composted or re-used.

ecological footprint: The measure of area needed to supply national populations with the resources and area needed to absorb their wastes.

ecology: The system of relationships between organisms and their environments.

economic impact (total): The total value of an event, including secondary spending (indirect and induced) on the host destination's local economy over and above the original direct spending. These secondary impacts, when combined with the original direct spending, result in the total economic impact of an event.

ecosystem: A community of living organisms interacting with themselves and with their environment.

ecotourism: Tourism that respects the culture, natural history and environment of destinations and seeks to minimize the negative impact of travel on the environment.

EDF Paper Calculator (Environmental Defense Fund):
http://www.edf.org/papercalculator/

endangered species/materials: A population of organisms that is at risk of becoming extinct because it is either few in number or threatened by changing environmental or predation parameters.

energy efficient: Using less energy to provide the same level of service.

Energy Star Equipment: A voluntary labeling program of the U.S. Environmental Protection Agency (EPA) and the U.S. Department of Energy that identifies energy-efficient products. Qualified products exceed minimum federal standards for energy consumption by a certain amount, or where no federal standards exist, have certain energy-saving features. Such products may display the Energy Star label.

energy/water conservation: Practices and strategies that are designed to minimize the amount of energy and water used.

environmental clause: A clause added to service provider contracts that stipulates requirements for environmental and sustainability practices and performance goals. It may also include concessions if the practices or goals are not met.

environmental criteria: Any set of parameters related to environmental practices, materials composition or participation in sustainability programs that is used to select and filter potential suppliers.

environmentally responsible transportation: Transportation options that minimize environmental impact such as mass public transportation (light rail, subway, electric/hybrid/biodiesel buses) and electric/hybrid vehicles.

environmental practices: Practices that encourage and maximize sustainability. Practices can be related to management, on-site activities, and supplier selection.

equal pay: A concept that states that individuals doing the same work should receive the same remuneration regardless of their gender, race, sexuality, nationality or anything else. Example of practical application: inquire at facility about outstanding union grievances.

ethical sourcing: The method of choosing products that take into account a company's responsibility for labor and human rights practices within all stages of its supply chain. Example of practical application: choosing fair trade coffee for your meeting.

evaluation: 1) Critiquing and rating the overall success of an event. 2) Developing an event profile from accurate event statistics. 3) A systematic process to determine the value of an activity.

event: An organized occasion such as a meeting, convention, exhibition, special event, gala dinner, etc. An event is often composed of several different yet related functions.

event organizer: Person whose job it is to oversee and arrange every aspect of an event. This person can be an employee or hired ad hoc to plan, organize, implement and control meetings, conventions and other events. See also *professional congress organizer, PCO.*

event site: Premises where an event will be held. See also *site*.

event specifications guide (ESG): The preferred term for a comprehensive document that outlines the complete requirements and instructions for an event. This document is typically authored by the event planner and is shared with all appropriate vendors as a vehicle to communicate the expectations of services for a project. The industry accepted practice is to use the APEX Event Specifications Guide, which can be found at the Convention Industry Council Web site. Sometimes called staging guide, resume.

event technology: Any technical and technology needs to support meetings or events. Includes items such as audiovisual, computers, software, power, networking and connectivity

e-waste: Waste materials generated from using or discarding electronic devices, such as computers, televisions, and mobile phones. E-waste tends to be highly toxic to humans, plants, and animals, and has been known to contaminate water, air and dirt.

exhibition: An event at which products, services or promotional materials are displayed to attendees visiting exhibits on the show floor. These events focus primarily on business-to-business (B2B) relationships.

exhibition manager: Preferred term for the specific person responsible for all aspects of planning, promoting and producing an exhibition. Also called show manager, show organizer. See also *show management, show producer.*

exhibitor: 1) Person or firm that displays its products or services at an event. 2) Event attendee whose primary purpose for attending the event is to staff a booth/stand.

exhibitor kit: See *exhibitor manual*.

exhibitor manual: Manual or kit, usually developed by the general service contractor for an event, containing general event information, labor/service order forms, rules and regulations and other information pertinent to an exhibitor's participation in an exhibition. Also called *exhibitor service kit*.

exhibitor service kit: See *exhibitor manual.*

facility: A structure that is built, installed, or established to serve a particular purpose. See also *convention center.*

fair: 1) Event principally devoted to the exhibition of agricultural products or industrial products. Fairs may also provide entertainment activities. 2) Exhibition of products or services in a specific area of activity held with the objective of promoting business.

fair trade: A market initiative to ensure that small farmers in developing countries are paid a fair market price that encourages independence and sustainability. Agricultural products may be fair trade certified.

Familiarization trip: Fam Trip. A program designed to acquaint potential buyers with specific destinations or services and to stimulate the booking of an event. Often offered in groups, but sometimes on an individual basis.

final program: Document containing the definitive conference and social program, circulated immediately prior to a conference or distributed at the commencement of the event.

fixed costs: The day-to-day cost of doing business that is pre-committed, such as salaries, insurance, lease expenses and utilities.

fossil fuel: An organic, energy-rich substance formed from the long-buried remains of prehistoric life.

fuel-efficient engine technology: Technologies that are recognized as those capable of making a significant impact on a car's overall fuel efficiency.

function: Any of a group of related organized occasions that contribute to a larger event.

general assembly: General and formal meeting of an organization or company attended by a specified proportion at least of its members for the purpose of deciding legislative direction, policy matters, the election of internal committees and approval of financial matters. An assembly generally observes certain fixed rules of procedure.

general service contractor (GSC): An organization that provides event management and exhibitors with a wide range of services, sometimes including, but not limited to, distributing the exhibitor manual, installation and dismantle, creating and hanging signage and banners, laying carpet, drayage, and providing booth/stand furniture. Also called official service sontractor. See also *decorator*.

general session: A meeting open to all those in attendance at an event. See *plenary session*.

global warming: A gradual, long-term increase in the near surface temperature of the earth. The term is most often used to refer to the warming predicted to occur as a result of increased emissions of greenhouse gases.

green: A common expression meaning environmentally responsible.

green collar job: A job connected to eco-friendly products and services.

greenhouse effect: Heating of the atmosphere that results from the absorption of solar radiation by certain gases.

greenhouse gas emissions: A gas that contributes to the greenhouse effect by absorbing solar radiation. These gases include, but are not limited to, carbon dioxide, ozone, methane and chlorofluorocarbons.

green meeting: According to APEX, a green meeting incorporates environmental considerations throughout all stages of the meeting in order to minimize the negative impact on the environment.

Green Seal Certified: An organization, product or process that has passed a specific environmentally responsible standard as outlined by Green Seal.

greenwash: To falsely claim a product is environmentally sound. Also known as faux green. Disinformation disseminated by an organization so as to present an environmentally conscious public image.

grey water reuse: The reuse of grey water, which is washwater. That is, all wastewater excepting toilet wastes and food wastes derived from garbage grinders.

gross square feet/meters: gsf or gsm. 1) Total amount of available function space in exhibit hall or other facility. 2) Total amount of space used for a specific show or event. See also *net square feet/meters*.

gross weight: The full weight of a shipment, including goods and packaging.

HAP: Stands for hazardous air pollutant.

hazmat: An abbreviation for hazardous material. A hazardous material is any item or agent (biological, chemical, physical) that has the potential to cause harm to humans, animals, or the environment, either by itself or through interaction with other factors.

high-efficiency speaker systems: These systems have cabinets that are typically smaller and lighter compared with older traditional models, thus requiring less truck space and ultimately allowing your sound provider to burn less fuel through greater fuel efficiency or by using smaller and fewer trucks. http://www.meetgreen.com/files/AVPrimer.pdf

hotel accommodation: Sleeping room(s) at a hotel and rooming arrangements, usually specifying the hotel classification in terms of its amenities, facilities, level of service and cost.

human rights: The basic rights and freedoms to which all humans are entitled regardless of race, nationality or membership in any particular social group. They specify the minimum conditions for human dignity and a tolerable quality of life. Example of practical application: ensure that the promotional products you purchase are sourced from a factory that has good working conditions (i.e., choose ethically sourced products). Resources: Human Rights Watch, Amnesty International and United Human Rights Council.

hybrid vehicle: Vehicle that uses a combination of two engine types. Cars are most commonly gasoline-electric hybrids.

in conjunction with (ICW): An event or function that occurs because of another event.

indirect costs: Also called overhead or administrative costs, these are expenses not directly related to the event. They can include salaries, rent, and building and equipment maintenance.

international: From outside the country where the event is hosted.

international event: 1) An event that draws a national and international audience. Typically 15% or more of attendees reside outside of the host country. 2) An event that draws an audience from three or more countries.

keynote: A session that opens or highlights the show, meeting or event.

keynote address: Opening remarks or presentation at a meeting that sets the tone or theme of the event and motivates attendees.

keynote speaker: Speaker whose presentation establishes the theme or tone of the event.

kilowatt hour: 1,000 watts of electricity used for one hour.

lamp recycling program: Recycling program specifically for fluorescent lamps, CFLs, and high-intensity discharge (HID) lamps, which contain small amounts of mercury.

LEED: Leadership in Energy and Environmental Design. A Green Building Rating System™ is a voluntary, consensus-based national standard for developing high-performance, sustainable buildings developed by the U.S. Green Building Council.

linen reuse program: Program in which a hotel or other type of accommodation facility asks their guests if they wish to have towels and/or sheets replaced each day. These programs conserve water, detergent and labor.

link: Using hypertext, a link is a selectable connection from one word, picture or information object to another. From a Web site, a link points to content.

liquid crystal display: LCD. Display composed of mobile crystals in liquid suspension that align themselves and polarize light in response to a small electric change. The crystals are manufactured in pockets within the display, which correspond to areas of dark on light background

living wages: A term used to describe the minimum hourly wage necessary for a person to achieve a quality of life generally higher than that indicated by the definition of poverty. Example of practical application: inquire if the facility supports its employees with a living wage. Resource: http://www.livingwage.geog.psu.edu/

local: From within 100 miles/160 kilometers or relevant local area such as a metropolitan area.

locally grown food: Food that is grown, produced and processed within 100 miles/160 kilometers of the event location.

locally recyclable: Items that can be recycled close to the event and do not require long distance transport to recycling facilities. For example, paper can often be recycled by local paper mills, whereas electronic equipment is usually shipped to other countries for recycling.

markup: Difference between the cost and the selling price of a given product. Difference between the net rate charged by a tour operator, hotel, or other supplier and the retail selling price of the service. Generally a percentage of the net rate rather than a fixed amount, as in a 20 percent markup on the net.

media kit: Packet of information that is supplied to the media; contains all the details of an event that are required to attract media attention and attendees.

meeting: An event where the primary activity of the participants is to attend educational sessions, participate in discussions, social functions, or attend other organized events. There is no exhibit component. Compare with *convention, exhibition, trade show, consumer show.*

meeting management company: A company, representing another organization, handling site selection, negotiations and turnkey support for an event.

meeting manager: See *planner*.

meeting profile: A written report outlining statistics of previous events, anticipated use of all services, profile of attendees, hotel occupancy patterns, etc.

metric system: A system of weights and measures, based on decimals, used throughout most of the world. Basic units are the gram for weight and the meter for length.

move-In/move-out dates: Dates set for installation/dismantling of an exhibition, a meeting, or other event.

multi-management firm: A company that offers complete turnkey organizational support for an event, including administrative and event management services.

national: From within the country where the event is hosted.

net square feet/meters: Also NSF. Actual amount of salable space used by exhibit booths/stands, which excludes aisles, lounges, registration areas, etc. See *gross square feet/meters (GSF or GSM)*.

news release: See *press release*.

no idling zones: Areas where buses and other commercial vehicle drivers are asked to not idle their vehicles. Engine idling wastes fuel, causes engine wear, and needlessly pollutes loading docks and other work sites with tailpipe exhaust.

objective: Formalized statement of outcomes to be anticipated as a result of the educational process.

occupancy sensor: A monitoring device, commonly connected to a room's lighting, but also occasionally to heating or ventilation, that shuts down these services when the space is unoccupied, thus saving energy.

offer: A promise, proposal or other expression of willingness to make and carry out a contract under proposed terms with another party that has the ability to accept it upon receiving it. Space and rent proposal from a facility. It may be in the form of a contract or license agreement.

offset energy use: Amount of energy use offset through purchase of offset credits.

off-site: A term that describes any function or activity that occurs away from the primary event facility. Examples of its use include off-site food and beverage, off-site venue.

on-site: A term that describes any function or activity that occurs at the primary event facility. See also *off-site.*

on-site management: Details that the event manager must supervise at the site of the event.

operations: Performing the practical work of operating a program. Usually involves the in-house control and handling of all phases of the services, both with suppliers and with clients.

operations manager: Individual in charge of performing the practical and detailed work of a program. See *operations.*

organic foods/certified organic: Grown without chemicals that can harm the land, water or human health. Organic certification of food can be through an independent organization or government program.

organizer: The entity or individual that produces an event.

organizing committee: A group of people who carry out the strategies and policies established for the organization of an event held in their geographic area.

outside vendor: Supplier who is not directly associated with the facility.

outsource: To subcontract a task or responsibility to a supplier to handle some aspect of an event, instead of using in-house staff.

Paper Calculator by EDF (Environmental Defense Fund):
http://www.edf.org/papercalculator/

participant: A person who is involved in an activity or event. This includes all persons at the event/meeting such as paid attendees, press, volunteers, staff and speakers.

PDA: An acronym for personal digital assistant.

percent of the gross: Type of payment involving a fixed percent of the gross income for that service. This type of agreement is often used by facilities as the rental rate.

percent of the net: Type of payment involving a fixed percent of the net income after costs of providing that service. This type of payment is often used in services provided by exclusive contractors within a facility.

per person: Goods or services priced and/or purchased according to the number of guests expected to attend the event.

pesticide: Any agent used to kill or control insects, weeds, rodents, fungi or other organisms.

planner: Person whose job it is to oversee and arrange every aspect of an event. Person can be employed by or hired ad hoc by companies, associations and other organizations to plan, organize, implement, and control meetings, conventions and other events.

planning matrix: A grid used to plan meeting formats and finalize subject areas, topics and assignments.

plastic laminate: Any one of several of the melamine plastics bonded to paneling for durability and appearance. Often used in exhibit construction.

plenary session: General assembly for all participants. See also *general session*.

post-conference: Any event that is arranged for the period immediately following the conference proper.

post-con meeting: Post-conference meeting at the primary facility at which an event occurred just after it has ended. Attendees generally include the primary event organizer, representatives of the event organizer/host organization, department heads at the facility, other facility staff as appropriate, and contractors. The agenda focuses on evaluating the implementation of the event and collecting data needed to complete an APEX Post-Event Report. It often includes a final review of bills with accounts payable. Compare with *pre-con meeting*.

post-consumer material/content: An end product that has completed its life cycle as a consumer item and would otherwise have been disposed of as solid waste. Post-consumer materials include recyclables collected in commercial and residential recycling programs, such as office paper, cardboard, aluminum cans, plastics and metals.

post-consumer recycled: Once a material or finished product has served its intended use and has been diverted or recovered from waste destined for disposal, it is then considered "post-consumer." Having completed its life as a consumer item, it can then be recycled as such. This differs from "pre-consumer" or "post-industrial" waste, which is generated by industrial or manufacturing waste.

post-consumer waste: Recycled material collected after people have tossed it in the blue bin. Office recycling programs and household recycling programs are the main source of post-consumer waste.

post-convention report: See *post-event report*.

poster board: Soft or cork board panel used for displaying copy and graphics.

post-event report: PER. The industry-preferred term for a report of the details and activities of an event. A collection of post-event reports over time will provide a comprehensive history for an event. The industry-accepted practice is to use the APEX Post-Event Report format, which can be found at the Convention Industry Council Web site.

post-event sustainability report: Report produced post-event summarizing sustainability measures and outcomes for an event.

pre-con meeting: A pre-conference meeting at the primary facility at which an event will take place just prior to the event beginning. Attendees generally include the primary event organizer, representatives of the event organizer/host organization, department heads at the facility, other facility staff as appropriate, and contractors. The agenda focuses on reviewing the purpose and details of the event and making final adjustments as needed. Compare with *post-con meeting*.

pre- or -post-event tour: Organized outing taking place before (pre-) or after (post-) an event for both attendees and accompanying persons.

press kit: A collection of publicity items that includes: 1) pertinent data on the meeting, such as agenda, historical data, guest speakers, special events, and the meeting property, such as descriptions of public space. 2) information relative to a sponsor's or exhibitor's products or services.

press release: 1) A prepared statement released to the news media. 2) An article intended for use by the media about a company, product, service, individual or show. Also called *news release.*

processed chlorine free (PCF): A bleaching process free of chlorine or chlorine compounds, which poisons rivers. The most common PCF bleaching agent is hydrogen peroxide (which breaks down into water and oxygen). Using PCF paper eliminates most of the toxic by-products of traditional bleaching, such as dioxins and other organochlorides, and this means cleaner rivers.

production company: A company that presents special effects and theatrical acts. This type of company may contract to put on an entire event or only parts of one. They sometimes hire speakers as part of their contract.

professional congress organizer (PCO): Companies or individuals specialized in organizing events on behalf of a client organization. Not to be confused with DMC (destination management company).

program: Schedule of events giving details of times and places.

program book: Printed schedule of events, location of function rooms, and other pertinent information.

program design: Structure of event program elements to achieve specific goals and objectives.

program development: Planning that takes place before an event regarding its specific content and fabric.

promotion: Publicizing an event. See *publicity*.

proposal: 1) Plan put forth for consideration or acceptance. 2) Communication sent by a supplier to a potential customer detailing the supplier's offerings and prices.

public relations: Presentation of an event via the media or other outlets, stressing the benefits and desirability of such event.

publicity: A media campaign, usually consisting of a series of public notices and advertising activities aimed at ensuring maximum attendance by focusing attention on an event. See *promotion*.

reception: Stand-up social function at which beverages and light foods are served. Foods may be presented on small buffet tables or passed by servers. May precede a meal function.

recycled paper: According to U.S. government standards, uncoated paper with at least 30% post-consumer waste and coated paper with at least 10% post-consumer waste can be called "recycled" paper.

recycling: The collection of waste materials and reprocessing them into new materials or products, which are then sold again.

refreshment break: Time between meeting sessions. May include coffee, soft drinks, and food items. Some are planned around a theme.

refreshments: Items of food and drink consumed between main meals, usually taken during breaks between meetings. See *break*.

regional event: An event targeted to attendees from a specific geographical area. May be a stand-alone event or a regional version of a national event. Typically, 60% of attendees reside within a 400-mile (640-km) radius of the event city.

registration: 1) Process by which an individual indicates his/her intent to attend a conference or stay at a property. 2) A method of booking and payment. 3) The process of recording data about an attendee (or exhibitor), sending a confirmation and creating a badge used on-site.

registration data: Information about an attendee that is gathered as part of the registration process (occupation, fee category, etc.).

registration fee: Amount payable for attendance at a conference, may vary according to level of participation or type of membership.

renewable energy: Renewable energy refers to energy derived from renewable sources such as water, solar, wind and geothermal heat. Renewable energy at the selected destination may refer to direct sources such as a convention center with solar panels, or indirect sources such as power off the grid sourced from a local wind farm. Select the option that most closely matches the availability of renewable energy at the location of your event.

renewable resources: Resources that are created or produced at least as fast as they are consumed, so that nothing is depleted. Includes solar, hydro, wind power, biomass and geothermal energy sources.

request for proposals (RFP): A document that stipulates what services the organization wants from an outside contractor and requests a bid to perform such services.

responsible seafood guide: Purchasing guide that lists various types of seafood with associated environmental impact, usually with a scale of low, medium and high impact. This also often takes into account endangered species in addition to farming and fishing practices. Several organizations produce these guides including SeaWeb, Blue Ocean Institute, Marine Conservation Society. Some guides are national and others refer to specific regions.

return on investment (ROI): 1) Net profit divided by net worth. A financial ratio indicating the degree of profitability. 2) Net benefits divided by the full loaded meeting costs.

rideshare program: The act or an instance of sharing motor vehicle transportation with another or others, especially among commuters, but this can also be coordinated for events.

sampling: A research method based on selecting a portion of a population for study.

satellite meeting: See *in conjunction with*.

service contractor: Outside company used by clients to provide specific products or services (e.g., pipe and drape, exhibitor manuals, floor plans, dance floors or flags). See also *general service contractor*.

service kit: See *exhibitor manual*.

shade-grown coffee: Coffee that is grown in the traditional manner, with coffee plants interspersed under a canopy of trees. End result: more habitats for birds, less need for chemical inputs, and the forest is not disrupted.

show management: The company, group or organization that manages an exhibition. See also *exhibition manager, show producer*.

show manager: See *exhibition manager*.

show organizer: See *exhibition manager*.

show producer: Company or individual who is responsible for all aspects of planning, promoting and producing an event. See also *exhibition manager, show manager*.

shuttle: A vehicle, usually a bus, contracted to transport event attendees between facilities during a certain time period.

shuttle service: Transportation for participants, usually by bus or van, provided on a continuous basis for a certain time period.

site: 1) Venue, area, location, property or specific facility to be used for an event. 2) A particular platform or location for loading or unloading at a place.

site inspection: In-person on-site review and evaluation of a venue or location for an event. See *familiarization trip*.

site selection: Choosing a venue for an event.

social/cultural factors: Factors related to interaction with other learners that affect the way a person learns.

social event: 1) An event with the purpose of facilitating pleasant companionship among attendees. 2) Life cycle celebration (e.g., a wedding, bar/bat mitzvah, anniversary, birthday, etc.). See *social program*.

social program: Program of organized functions, not directly related to the main educational subject of an event. See *social event*.

sustainability: Meeting the needs of the present without compromising the ability of future generations to meet their own needs (as defined by the Brundtland Commission, 1987).

sustainability commitment: A sustainability commitment can include any written or oral statements by the city administration that indicate a commitment toward making sustainability a priority. Sustainability can refer to environmental, social or economic sustainability.

sustainability criteria: Any set of parameters related to environmental practices, materials composition or participation in sustainability programs that is used to select and filter potential suppliers.

sustainability policy: Set of guidelines related to policy, generally written, which outline an organization's commitment and practices related to sustainability.

sustainable flooring options: Flooring made from sustainable, renewable or recycled sources. Made of recycled carpet, certified wood.

sustainable food: Food that is healthy for consumers and animals, does not harm the environment, is humane for workers, respects animals, provides a fair wage for the farmer, and supports and enhances rural communities.

sustainable transportation: Sustainable transportation includes public transit, hybrid shuttles and taxis, ride share services and bike share services.

switch mode power supply: These are highly energy-efficient, lighter-weight, and cooler operating components. Examples of excellent amplifiers that fit a high-efficiency standard include "Lab Gruppen FP+ or PLM" series, and "QSC PL 2 or 3" series. Another amplifier option is to utilize four-channel amplifiers if possible, which are able to deliver essentially twice the utility that an older two-channel amp would provide but in the same amount of space. http://www.meetgreen.com/files/AVPrimer.pdf

teleconference: Type of meeting that brings together three or more people in two or more locations through telecommunications.

third party: A person other than the principals.

third-party certified in sustainability: LEED, Green Seal, BS 8901, ISO14001, state certifications. Third-party certification means that an independent entity (usually the certifying body itself) has reviewed and confirmed sustainability practices. There is no definitive list of third-party certifications, so verify the claims of accommodations suppliers with regard to participating in certifications by confirming that they are indeed third parties.

time line: Includes each task to be accomplished and is the core of the program plan.

trade fair: An international term for an exhibition.

trade-out: A type of barter. The exchange of goods and services instead of using money.

trade show: An exhibition of products and/or services held for members of a common or related industry. Not open to the general public. See *exhibition*. Compare with *consumer show*.

total energy use: Total energy consumed by an event. May include meeting venues, off-site venues and accommodations usage.

toxic materials: Toxic materials are substances that may cause harm to an individual through direct contact, inhalation and/or consumption.

trawling: Also known as dredging, the process of dragging huge, heavy nets over the sea floor, scooping up everything in their path.

triple bottom line: A business and development philosophy incorporating the three E's: equity, environment, economics. Also referred to as the three P's: people, planet, profit.

variable costs or expenses: Expenses that vary based upon various factors, such as the number of attendees.

vegan: Lifestyle choice that excludes the consumption and use of animal flesh and by-products.

vegetable-based Inks: Environmentally friendly printing inks that are made from vegetable oils combined with pigments. The most common type is made from soy.

vegetarian: Dietary choice that excludes the consumption of animal flesh or by-products, but may include eggs and dairy.

venue: 1) Site or destination of meeting, event or show. 2) Location of performance such as hall, ballroom, auditorium, etc.

very important person (VIP): Person who has a special function at the event (speaker, dignitary, etc.) and should be treated with special care and attention.

videoconference: A meeting between two or more people or groups across a distance, including video, audio, and potentially other data, utilizing telecommunications or communications satellites for transmission of the signal. See *teleconference*.

virgin paper: Paper manufactured from new pulp or cotton. Does not contain any recycled material.

virtual conferencing: Any meeting where people at two or more distant locations are linked using video, audio and data for two-way communication via satellite communications or the Internet. Each party sees and hears the other through a TV screen or computer monitor and audio speakers.

virtual tour: Any tour where people at two or more distant locations are linked using video, audio and data for communications. Each party sees and hears the tour through a TV screen or computer monitor and audio speakers.

virtual trade show: Exhibit of products or services that can be viewed over the Internet.

volatile organic compounds (VOC): Compounds that have a high vapor pressure and low water solubility. Many VOCs are human-made chemicals used and produced in the manufacture of paints, pharmaceuticals and refrigerants. VOCs typically are industrial solvents, such as trichloroethylene; fuel oxygenates, such as methyl tert-butyl ether (MTBE); or by-products produced by chlorination in water treatment, such as chloroform. VOCs are often components of petroleum fuels, hydraulic fluids, paint thinners and dry cleaning agents. VOCs are common ground water contaminants.

walking distance: Hotel rooms located within five city blocks or accessible by public transportation to the convention center or meeting venue.

walk-through: 1) Review of event details. 2) Site inspection. 3) Inspection of function room prior to function. 4) Inspection of exhibit floor prior to opening of the event.

webcast: An event that broadcasts the audio and/or video portion of a keynote presentation or other educational sessions over the Web in real-time or on-demand.

webconferencing: Web browser-based videoconferencing.

whiteboarding: A feature of videoconferencing systems that allows the placement of shared documents on an on-screen shared space or "whiteboard." Participants can edit and mark up the document just as on a physical whiteboard.

zero-based budgeting: The process of building a budget without benefit of a previous year's budget.

Authors

Nancy J. Zavada

Nancy J. Zavada is the founding principal of MeetGreen®, which she established in 1994. She has been internationally recognized as an author, speaker, leader, innovator and entrepreneur in the sustainable meetings and events management industry. Nancy served on the Live Earth Global Green Team and was twice named one of "The 25 Most Powerful People in the Meetings Industry" by MeetingNews Magazine and was presented with the "Achievement for Innovation in Hospitality" award by the Institute for Innovation and Economic Development. She is co-founder of the Green Meeting Industry Council (GMIC) and served on the Green Meeting Task Force for PCMA. Nancy is co-author of "Simple Steps to Green Meetings and Events: The Professional's Guide to Saving Money and the Earth." In her blog, "Pretentious Musings of a Meet Green Martyr," she shares resources, tips and ideas for green meeting planners.

Amy Spatrisano

Amy Spatrisano is a principal of MeetGreen®. She has an international reputation in the sustainable meeting and events management field as a pioneer, leader, speaker, visionary and innovator. She has been named one of "The 25 Most Powerful People in the Meetings Industry," has been acknowledged as one of the "Growing Green Leaders," was included in the list of "Eco-Leaders" and was presented with the "Achievement for Innovation in Hospitality" award by the Institute for Innovation and Economic Development. She is co-founder of the Green Meeting Industry Council (GMIC) and served as the APEX Panel Chair to develop the APEX/ASTM Environmentally Sustainable Meeting Standards and served on the Live Earth Global Green Team. She co-authored the book "Simple Steps to Green Meetings and Events: The Professional's Guide to Saving Money and the Earth" and is currently a member of the working group for the Global Reporting Initiative's Event Organizers Sector Supplement.

Shawna McKinley

Named the "Green Queen" and "Green Leader to Watch" by Meetingsnet.com, Shawna McKinley's dedication to the environment and to the meeting industry is made even more obvious in her list of association affiliations, task force participation and speaking engagements. She has served as the Executive Director of the Green Meeting Industry Council (GMIC), as General Manager of Ocean Blue Foundation, on the APEX-ASTM Environmentally Sustainable Meeting Standards development panel and on the Convention Industry Council's Green Meeting Task Force. She has a degree in Tourism Management with a Major in Regional and Urban Planning and a Master of Arts in Environmental Education and Communication. She is currently the Director of Sustainability at MeetGreen®, where she continues to encourage and educate the meeting industry in sustainability practices.

Company Information

MeetGreen®
Connect. Sustain. Thrive.

Based in Portland, Oregon, MeetGreen® works with progressive organizations worldwide to integrate sustainable meetings practices into the events it produces and assesses while delivering targeted business results. Since its founding in 1994, MeetGreen® has embraced sustainability as a defining core value. MeetGreen®'s mission is to continuously transform the meetings industry through leadership, innovation, education and performance inspired by social and environmental responsibility to the planet and the people on it.

Connect. Sustain. Thrive.
www.meetgreen.com | info@meetgreen.com